BEHAVIOURAL SCIENCE FOR MARKETING AND BUSINESS STUDENTS

Joseph MacDonagh
and
Rebecca Weldridge

GILL & MACMILLAN

Published in Ireland by
Gill & Macmillan Ltd
Goldenbridge
Dublin 8
with associated companies throughout the world
© Joseph MacDonagh and Rebecca Weldridge 1994
0 7171 2164 X
Designed by Elaine Shiels
Index compiled by Helen Litton
Print origination by Seton Music Graphics, Bantry, Co. Cork
Printed by ColourBooks Ltd, Dublin

CONTENTS

Foreword

Introduction

1. Behavioural Science   1

2. Perception   16

3. Learning and Memory   39

4. Motivation   56

5. Attitudes   77

6. Personality   104

7. Groups   121

8. Organisations and Organisational Behaviour   144

9. Culture and Society   168

10. Trends in Irish Social Change   179

References   190

Index   195

FOREWORD

As psychologists lecturing in the areas of management and marketing, we became acutely aware of the need for a textbook which dealt with the basic behavioural science concepts and theories in a straightforward and jargon-free manner. This book caters for students of business courses (whether sales, advertising, marketing or management) and of other non-psychology subjects involving aspects of human behaviour.

We have counteracted the bias inherent in many textbooks used in Irish courses, which focus exclusively on American or British examples. As well as making it more neutral, we have ensured that the book is easily accessible for student learning and reference. Each chapter begins with 'learning objectives', has clearly defined section headings, contains summaries in point form and ends with possible exam questions (some drawn from professional bodies' past papers).

We believe we have explained simply and accurately the theories of behavioural sciences.

Joseph MacDonagh MA   Rebecca Weldridge MA
Business School   School of Business & Marketing
RTC Tallaght   College of Marketing and Design
Dublin   Dublin

INTRODUCTION

Behavioural science is the study of people and their behaviour. We review the principles of the science, with each chapter addressing a different issue, as follows:

Chapter 1 is a general **introductory section** which explains what behavioural science actually is, how it tries to attain the goals of a science and how it uses scientific methodology to collect and collate data in order to produce objective results.

Chapter 2 examines the issue of **perception**, i.e. how we see the world around us. As we are unique we differ in our outlooks. We investigate the way in which processes of perceptual selection and organisation contribute towards this difference. Finally, we discuss social perception, and how we view and relate to other people.

Chapter 3 concentrates on **learning and memory** theories. We focus on two different theories. One proposes that learning behaviour is merely a case of conditioning; the other claims that learning involves higher mental processes such as insight and understanding. The former is the behaviourist, the latter the cognitive approach. This chapter also examines memory, how we remember, how we forget and what mechanisms we use to memorise material.

Chapter 4 considers a number of **motivational theories**. We investigate theorists such as Maslow, McClelland and others whose works are used in today's business world. The understanding of motivation is as important for those who manage as for those who are managed.

Chapter 5 identifies the complex components and functions of **attitudes**. We look at how people acquire attitudes, the effect they have on behaviour and how they change. We examine a number of attitudinal theories and present their applications within marketing and organisational spheres.

Chapter 6 discusses four approaches to **personality** theory, ranging from the psychodynamic (Sigmund Freud and Carl Gustav Jung) to the nurturing (Carl Rogers) and trait (Raymond Cattell) approaches.

Chapter 7 sees a change in orientation from the individual to **the group**. This chapter examines the make-up, development and functions of groups. The impact of group influence on individual behaviour is also reviewed.

Chapter 8 investigates **organisational life**; how organisations are structured, their technological and recruitment approaches and employee–employer relationships.

Chapter 9 focuses on the concepts of **culture and society**, and the influence of both on human behaviour. As the three are inextricably linked, it is impossible to study human behaviour without this broad societal perspective.

Chapter 10 looks at the dramatic changes in **Irish society** over the past forty years in terms of social and industrial demographics. We also discuss the major trends in Irish society, and the way in which its primary influences still exert a strong 'pull' on our consciousness. This chapter should be considered only a starting-point for a study of the subject, as a definitive examination is outside the nature and scope of this text.

1

1

Behavioural Science

1.1   INTRODUCTION

1.2   WHY DO WE STUDY BEHAVIOURAL SCIENCE?

1.3   WHAT IS BEHAVIOURAL SCIENCE?
1.3.1 Natural science vs. behavioural science

1.4   HOW DO WE STUDY BEHAVIOURAL SCIENCE?
1.4.1 Forming the research question
1.4.2 Methodologies
1.4.3 Validity
1.4.4 Scales of measurement
1.4.5 Problems of behavioural science, in claiming to be a science

1.5   SUMMARY

1.6   EXAM QUESTIONS

Learning Objectives

After studying this chapter you should be able to:

— *Understand the discipline of behavioural science and its applications in the real world*
— *Identify the problems of behavioural science in claiming to be a science*
— *Understand the ways in which behavioural scientists apply systematic and objective analysis to their work*
— *Discuss the five basic research design methodologies*
— *Summarise the scales of measurement used within behavioural science.*

1.1 INTRODUCTION

We examine here the genesis, nature and applications of behavioural science, and ask:

(a)   Why do we study behavioural science?
(b)   What does it involve?
(c)   How do we study it?

Throughout the book we use examples from business, marketing and real life to highlight a particular point or clarify a principle, in order to show how the theories of behavioural science are applicable in all three areas.

1.2 WHY DO WE STUDY BEHAVIOURAL SCIENCE?

Marketers need a comprehensive knowledge of behavioural science to acquire insights into consumer behaviour. As noted by Chisnall (1985), a consumer behaviour theorist, 'buying behaviour should take account of the structure of society and the interactions of individuals within the various groups and subgroups . . . cultural beliefs, values . . . '.

Consumerism is an interactive variable in the overall pattern of people's behaviour. For example, food and clothing frequently have social rather than solely functional values. Food can be used to enhance prestige; clothing can express status and personality. **Augmented product or service** is a concept often utilised by the marketing industry, which recognises buyer behaviour as a complex dynamic comprising many psychological factors, such as perceptions, motivations and attitudes. In today's world it is necessary for marketers to understand the importance of the underlying factors affecting behaviour. The emphasis on customer satisfaction is as much psychological as it is physical.

From an organisational perspective, behavioural science principles are of tremendous importance, as organisations consist of people and their often complex behaviours. A knowledge of this science may help management to:

(a) understand how employee attitudes and motivations affect interaction within the workplace

(b) understand the importance of psychological and social influences on employee performance levels

(c) understand the need for specific interpersonal skills in the appraisal or disciplining of staff.

Ineffective management leads to organisational mediocrity and perhaps failure. Effective management, incorporating behavioural science principles, helps an organisation to function at its optimum level.

Human behaviour does not occur in a vacuum. The causes of our behaviour are a combination of personal condition and social interaction. As society becomes increasingly complex, the need to understand behavioural principles becomes more apparent. Unless we learn why people behave as they do, we cannot hope to understand them. By nature we are curious, not only about ourselves but also about our fellow beings. We are avid people-watchers; their behaviour perplexes and fascinates us. In the following chapters we identify some of the causes of human behaviour.

1.3 WHAT IS BEHAVIOURAL SCIENCE?

Behavioural science is a collective noun encompassing disciplines such as psychology, sociology, anthropology and economics — four distinct topics in their own right, yet complementary to the study of human behaviour.

Psychology studies human and animal behaviour with the ultimate goal of gathering knowledge for the benefit of humanity. It seeks to determine the causes of behaviour, i.e. motives, attitudes and how individuals learn and modify responses to their environment. Psychologist Henry James (1890) defined psychology as the 'science of mental life'.

Sociology studies social structures, trends and the collective behaviour of individuals in groups. Of particular interest is the social influence of a group over individuals in terms of norms, status and power.

Anthropology studies the cultural determinants of human behaviour, focusing particularly on the demands of society which shape individual and group behaviour.

Economics studies the interaction of production, exchange and consumption of goods and services.

We focus mainly on the first discipline, psychology, in order to comprehend how and why individuals relate to each other and their environment. We borrow from sociology and anthropology where those disciplines enhance our understanding of the collective nature of people in terms of cultural and social influences, and we use some economic data in analysing the changes in Irish society over the last forty-odd years.

Before proceeding further we must define some important concepts and terms integral to behavioural science.

Variable

The concept of a variable is central to the discipline and is any entity which can vary. Behavioural science recognises two:

independent variables are the suspected cause of behaviour in an experiment

dependent variables reveal the effect of the independent variables.

These are discussed later in the chapter.

Quantitative and qualitative research

Most behavioural research is quantitative, i.e. we observe a variable and then quantify or measure it. Qualitative research involves asking subjects of experiments about their feelings. Quantitative research asks subjects to complete questionnaires with *closed* questions, responding yes or no (e.g. 'Do you think there is too much unemployment in the country?'). In qualitative research the respondents are asked *open* questions which elicit feelings or opinions (e.g. 'Why do you think unemployment is so high?'). Quantitative research measures the extent or degree of a behaviour, while qualitative research indicates reasons for particular behaviours.

Sampling

One must recognise the statistical notion of a **sample** drawn from a test population. Francis (1988) notes:

> In practice, most of the information obtained by organisations about any population will come from examining a small, representative subset of the population. This is called a sample. For example (a) a company might examine one in every twenty of their invoices for a month to determine the average amount of a customer order; (b) a newspaper might commission a research company to ask 1,000 potential voters their opinions on a forthcoming election. The information gathered from a sample (i.e. measurements, facts and/or opinions) will normally give a good indication of the measurements, facts and/or opinions of the population from which it was drawn.

The more representative the sample, and the closer in size it is to the population, the more accurate it is likely to be. This introduces the notion of validity, examined later in the chapter.

1.3.1 Natural science vs. behavioural science

As noted by the psychologist E.G. Boring (Schultz, 1982), the application of the scientific method to the study of the mind is the greatest event in the history of psychology. If behavioural scientists believe that scientific methodology is the only route to an objective understanding of human behaviour, they must systematically study behaviour using the principles and methods of scientific research.

Science is often thought of as a body of knowledge that is more objective than knowledge not scientific. Natural sciences such as chemistry, physics and biology are relatively easy to study in terms of measurement and control, with causal relationships being observed through experimentation and hypothesis (proposition) testing.

Science is a discipline dedicated to objectivity and evaluation. It has four goals:

Description: This involves the labelling, defining and classifying of objects, events, situations, and observable relationships between the above.

Understanding: Attempting to discover what causes a particular effect between variables.

Prediction: Accurate prediction (a) has practical value and (b) affords a test of understanding.

Control: Control over the method of inquiry is necessary, particularly: (a) events that take place in the experiment; (b) extraneous variables (factors not being specifically researched) that could contaminate results; (c) when and how behaviours under study will be measured.

The goals of science are complementary. Description opens doors to understanding while prediction and control index the accuracy of our understanding.

Goals of Science

description	—	defining
understanding	—	cause & effect
prediction	—	accuracy
control	—	measurement

If behavioural science wishes to call itself a science, how does it (a) attain the goals of a science and (b) construct an objective method of inquiry?

1.4 HOW DO WE STUDY BEHAVIOURAL SCIENCE?

1.4.1 Forming the research question

Behavioural scientists have to describe and explain real-life responses through examining real-life events, testing their data against reality. They must map out a sequence of activities that meets the requirements of a scientific investigation. It can be summarised as follows:

Step 1: **Formulate the question** to be asked — what is to be studied?

Step 2: **Operationalise the question** by translating it into an appropriate research design — decide on the most appropriate manner of investigation.

Step 3: **Measure the behaviour** of interest — observation of subjects under specific conditions and conversion of responses into numerical data.

Step 4: **Extract relationships** from data through the use of logic and statistics — control and measurement being vital for reliability.

Step 5: **Interpret relationships** with due consideration for theoretical implications.

Step 6: Decide whether the research design used and conclusions reached are **generalisable and repeatable**.

One of the major concerns of research is how to operationalise the research question: in other words, how to decide on the best methodology. The research design is selected on three criteria:

(a) nature of the question — is it easily operationalised?

(b) practical considerations — what will the problems be?

(c) purpose of the study — will the design disclose the type of information required?

1.4.2 Methodologies

Five basic research methods are used in behavioural science. No one method is sufficient for researching all psychological topics; frequently a mixture of methods offers the best solutions. Methods differ from one another in the degree to which the researcher intervenes and changes the environment of his subjects. One of the main research objectives is to control variables that bear on internal validity (see section 1.4.3).

The most common research methods are:

Systematic observation: This develops an accurate description of behaviours and relationships of people who are not aware of being observed: in other words, natural and unobtrusive observation of unaware subjects in their natural environment by the researcher. This design generally involves the least researcher intervention, e.g. observing subjects through a two-way mirror or video film in a supermarket security camera.

Case-study: This is an intensive investigation focusing on past and present behaviours to establish a relationship between the two. The subject is aware of being studied as research is by self-report and interview. Researcher intervention and control are higher than in systematic observation, and the method is open to more subjective interpretation by the scientist. It was used extensively by Freud.

Psychometric method: A sample of people is given one or more psychological tests and measured on two or more psychological traits. A statistical analysis is performed on test scores to see if a correlation exists between the scores on one trait (e.g. intelligence) and the scores on another (e.g. reading ability). This method investigates the relationship between the possession of two traits.

Researcher intervention is high.

Survey method: Surveys are conducted on samples of people to generalise to whole populations. Surveys tend to be conducted:

(a) by definition of population and variables of study, e.g. surveying women (population) on their choice of perfume (variable)

(b) by drawing a representative sample of people from the defined population, e.g. selecting a balanced number from various areas, ages, and occupations

(c) by measuring the target variables in the sample, e.g. how many women actually purchase the perfume

(d) on the basis of the sample variables, attempting general statements about the original population's variable, e.g. the amount purchased gives an idea of how popular the perfume is with women generally.

Researcher intervention is necessary but control is quite low, especially in the case of postal surveys.

Experimental method: This is possibly the most efficient method available to the behavioural scientist. Let us take the example of investigating the effect of alcohol on driving ability. One independent variable (alcohol) is manipulated while all other potential influences are held constant. The dependent variable (driving ability) is observed and recorded. If this behaviour changes significantly, the change may be logically attributed to the one variable (the independent, e.g. amount of alcohol consumed) that was deliberately varied. Although this is an efficient and popular method there are considerable problems to overcome.

(a) Extraneous variables are hard to control i.e. it is impossible to control the entire environment.

(b) Subjects may behave atypically (not in their usual manner because of being studied).

(c) Laboratory-type setting is artificial and unnatural.

(d) Experimental study may often be unrealistically simple in an effort to aid research.

Observation and measurement are important concepts in behavioural science methods. Observation is important because it provides systematic recording of behaviour that falls into pre-selected behavioural categories. Measurement is important because it involves using an unambiguous set of rules to convert these observations into a numerical scale. Behavioural science uses logic, observation and measurement to translate psychological concepts into observable behaviours, then into numbers, which in turn can be subjected to statistical analysis.

Behavioural Science Methodologies

Systematic observation
Case-study
Psychometric
Survey
Experimental

1.4.3 Validity

Any experimental research must fulfil the assumption of validity, i.e. that the research is actually studying what it says it is. There are two basic types of validity:

Internal validity refers to the interpretation of internal relationships. An investigation has internal validity to the extent that changes in the independent variable (the variable thought to influence, determine or cause change in other variables) can be deemed responsible for changes in the dependent variable (the specific behaviour observed or measured). For example, what effect does intelligence (independent variable) have on academic success (dependent variable)? In a study like this there would probably be high internal validity.

External validity refers to the extent to which the findings of one particular study can be generalised to other populations and settings. Taking the above example, is the finding amongst the sample of schoolchildren generalisable to the entire population of Irish schoolchildren?

Behavioural science researchers recognise the inherent difficulty in attaining a balance between internal and external validity, as findings from a (hopefully) representative sample are not always true for the entire population.

1.4.4 Scales of measurement

It is important for behavioural scientists to select the appropriate scale of measurement for a research design, one which accurately reflects the amount of data collected. The scale employed determines the mathematical and statistical operations which can be performed on the data. Generally, scientific disciplines distinguish between four levels or scales of measurement: nominal, ordinal, interval and ratio.

Nominal represents the lowest level of measurement, where observations are sorted into categories representing differences or similarities in kind. This scale makes only qualitative distinctions, i.e. male/female. There is no indication of differences in magnitude or quantity. Using this scale limits statistical treatments of data.

Ordinal permits an ordering of observations according to magnitude; this is a quantitative scale allowing assignment of numbers to observations to represent different amounts of a characteristic. Ordinal scales provide information on 'more' or 'less', i.e. Grade A is higher than Grade B, which is higher than Grade C. There is, however, no indication of the amount of distance between Grades: for example, Grade A is not necessarily twice as good as B, nor B twice as good as C. This scale provides information on the relative positions of observations on a measured dimension but not information on the distance between observations.

For the final two levels of measurement we quote from Hair et al. (1992):

> **Interval and ratio scales** provide the highest level of measurement precision. Thus they permit nearly all mathematical operations to be performed. These two scales have constant units of measurement, so differences between two adjacent points on any part of the scales are equal. The only real difference between interval and ratio scales is that interval scales have an arbitrary zero point, while ratio scales have an absolute zero point.

The most familiar interval scales are the Fahrenheit and Celsius temperature scales. Both have a different arbitrary zero point, and neither indicates a zero amount or lack of temperature, since we can register temperatures below the zero point of each scale. Therefore, it is not possible to say that any value on an interval scale is some multiple of some other point on the scale. For example, an 80°F day cannot correctly be said to be twice as hot as a 40°F day because we know that 80°F, using a different scale, such as Celsius, is 26.7°C. Similarly, 40°F, using Celsius, is 4.4°C. Although 80°F is indeed twice 40°F, one cannot state that the heat of 80°F is twice the heat of 40°F because, using different scales, the heat is not twice as great, that is 4.4°C x 2 ≠ 26.7°C.

Ratio scales represent the highest form of measurement precision, since they possess the advantages of all lower scales plus an absolute zero point. All mathematical operations are allowable with ratio scale measurements. The bathroom scale or other common weighing machines are examples of these scales, for they have an absolute zero point and can be spoken of in terms of multiples when relating one point on the scale to another; for example, 100 pounds is twice as heavy as 50 pounds.

1.4.5 Problems of behavioural science, in claiming to be a science

If behavioural scientists want to study behaviour scientifically they must attain the goals of science. Immediately problems spring to mind. How is it possible to measure aspects of the human character? How is it possible to predict outcomes when people behave irrationally? Perhaps most importantly, how is it possible to remain objective when interpretation itself is a subjective process?

Human behaviour is rarely straightforward. Unlike natural science variables, people are constantly changing. The very topic of study or interest is often non-observable. For example, how is it possible to study people's perceptions of a particular event when perception itself is a hypothetical construct, i.e. an unseen process.

The following table highlights behavioural science problems attached to each scientific goal.

GOAL	PROBLEM
DESCRIPTION (observation and measurement)	(a) **Deals with intangibles** (e.g. attitudes, motivation, perceptual processes)
	(b) **Multiplicity of variables** (e.g. people usually behave in a particular way for a combination of reasons)
	(c) **Precision is often elusive** (e.g. there may be a great deal of error due to the test or tester used)
	(d) **Behaviour may be unquantifiable** (e.g. how to measure motivation in people)
	(e) **Objectivity is difficult** (e.g. when dealing with behaviours we find personally distasteful, such as racism)
UNDERSTANDING (cause and effect)	(a) **Often non-observable** (e.g. perception and motivation are both internal and unseen processes)
	(b) **Unpredictability of human behaviour** (e.g. there is no guarantee human beings will act consistently in a given situation)
	(c) **Unreliability of relationships** (e.g. while we may establish a link between two experimental behaviours, frequently results are not replicated)
PREDICTION (outcomes)	(a) **Irrationality of humans** (e.g. humans are original and at times completely irrational in response to rational requests)
	(b) **Susceptible to research bias** (e.g. it can be tempting for researchers to influence outcomes in order to 'prove' their hypothesis)

(c) **Internal variables susceptible to change** (e.g. due to the effect of different mood states and emotions, subjects' responses are not always predictive)

(d) **Complexity and uniqueness of the individual** (e.g. no two people are alike, each will respond in his own unique fashion)

CONTROL

(a) **Ethical and moral constraints** (e.g. behavioural scientists are bound by professional guidelines not to inflict mental or physical pain on human beings. This affects the range of work which can be carried out on human beings, especially as these guidelines prohibit potentially harmful deception on the part of the experimenter.)

(b) **Unforeseen extraneous variables** (e.g. the experimenters may have designed their experiment in the belief that certain conditions would apply. If these conditions change because of the effect of unforeseen, or extraneous, variables, the accuracy of results will be affected.)

(c) **Attempted manipulation of individuals by researcher** (e.g. though this seldom occurs, an experimenter may decide to choose individuals, or may influence people unduly, so that a particular result is achieved)

This chapter has provided a general introduction to the discipline of behavioural science. Its pursuance of a scientific path of inquiry gives it a platform for establishing a credible explanation of cause and effect — or the 'why' of human behaviour.

1.5 SUMMARY

1. Behavioural science is a collective concept encompassing disciplines such as psychology, sociology, anthropology and economics.
2. It is a science which attempts to remove personal bias and preconceptions from interpretation of human behaviour by using the scientific method of inquiry.
3. It attempts to attain the goals of science: description, understanding, prediction and control.
4. It uses five basic research designs: systematic observation, case-study, psychometric method, survey method and experimental method.
5. Four scales of measurement are employed to aid statistical interpretation of data: nominal, ordinal, interval and ratio.

1.6 EXAM QUESTIONS

1. Briefly describe the goals of science and discuss the problems behavioural science may encounter when attaining such goals.
2. From a management perspective, list the advantages gained from a knowledge of behavioural science.
3. Explain the concept of validity within research design.
4. Evaluate the various scientific methodologies of data collection.
5. What measurement scales are used by behavioural scientists?

Perception

2.1   INTRODUCTION

2.2   SENSATION
2.2.1 What is sensation?
2.2.2 Thresholds
2.2.3 Habituation

2.3   PERCEPTUAL SELECTIVITY
2.3.1 Selection process
2.3.2 External cues
2.3.3 Internal cues

2.4   PERCEPTUAL ORGANISATION
2.4.1 Organisation of stimuli
2.4.2 Laws of Gestalt

2.5   INDIVIDUAL'S PERCEPTUAL WORLD
2.5.1 Unique views
2.5.2 Categorisation
2.5.3 Perceptual expectancies
2.5.4 Selective perception
2.5.5 Perceptual defence
2.5.6 Attribution

2.6   SOCIAL PERCEPTION
2.6.1 Views of others
2.6.2 Characteristics of person perceived
2.6.3 Characteristics of perceiver
2.6.4 Characteristics of situation
2.6.5 Influencing factors

2.7   SUMMARY

2.8   EXAM QUESTIONS

Learning Objectives

After studying this chapter you should be able to:

— *Define the processes of perception and sensation*
— *Describe the perceptual selectivity process with its accompanying perceptual cues*
— *Discuss perceptual organisation, with particular reference to Gestalt laws*
— *Understand an individual's perceptual world along with its influencing factors*
— *Identify the salient variables that influence social perception.*

2.1 INTRODUCTION

Often viewed as a single process, perception actually consists of several distinct processes. Perception is interpretation. We do not have access to an objective reality, we have only an interpretative reality. That is, our reality is as *we* perceive it to be.

Perception is frequently defined as the process by which an individual selects, organises and interprets sensory stimuli into a meaningful picture of the world. In other words, perception is the way we 'see' the world around us. Because human phenomena are extraordinary states, we are all remarkably different and complex individuals. It is logical therefore that we should each have a differing perception; what one person perceives as meaningful another may perceive as false.

The perceptual process is common to us all, and we use it to make sense of our environment. We must understand what is going on in order to assess and select the appropriate behavioural response in any particular situation. A person's perception of a situation is not necessarily accurate, but it is that person's portrayal of the event.

This unique portrait is influenced by many variables or factors. For example, past experiences, motivations and expectations all have an effect on the perceiver. As noted by Kretch et al. (1962), an individual's perception of a given situation 'is not then a photographic representation of the physical world; it is, rather, a partial, personal construction'. A knowledge of the perceptual process is fundamental to understanding human behaviour. If we can understand how individuals view their world, we can begin to understand why they behave as they do.

This chapter has five main sections. First, we discuss the concept of sensation and how it leads into the perceptual process. Second, we examine perceptual selectivity, how individuals select and at times dismiss environmental cues. Third, we look at the process of perceptual organisation, how selected cues are organised in such a way as to aid understanding and interpretation. Fourth, we investigate an individual's perceptual world and the processes that contribute to their own picture of the world. Finally, we describe social perception, the process whereby individuals make judgments and form opinions of others.

Within a marketing sphere, an understanding of the perceptual process is important as consumers act/react on the basis of their perceptions, not on the basis of objective reality. Frequently products or services have a symbolic value for consumers, reflecting both their perceived self-image and the perceived product image. Consumers often buy a product in the belief that it will enhance their perceived self-image (buying a celebrity-endorsed perfume) or that by buying a perceived 'status' product, the status is in some way transferred to them. A knowledge of perceptual intricacies can aid marketers in determining what influences buying behaviour.

From an organisational viewpoint an understanding of perception benefits management–employee relationships in a number of ways. For example, it ensures there is a shared interpretation of organisational goals, it helps to avoid inappropriate stereotyping judgments and opinions during selection and appraisal procedures, and it enhances awareness of management and employee perceptual defence mechanisms.

Even in everyday situations, a knowledge of perception helps us to comprehend and cope with life. If we are aware of the process, we can be aware of how different cues trigger our attention and affect behaviour. We can begin to understand what causes us and others to see a situation in a particular way, and how people in general are very quick to form judgments and attribute causes to behaviours.

2.2 SENSATION

2.2.1 What is sensation?

We cannot have perception without first experiencing sensation. Sensation may be defined as the immediate and direct response of the sensory organs to simple stimuli.

A stimulus is anything that rouses a person to activity or produces a reaction in an organ or tissue of the body. The human body is equipped with five receptors through which it receives sensory data:

Receptor	Data
eyes	visual
ears	auditory
mouth	oral
skin	tactile
nose	smell

The information received results in a corresponding sensation.

Sensation and perception co-exist. We need to be aware of stimuli before we can interpret them. Every day we are bombarded with vast amounts of internal and external information: hunger or thirst (internal stimuli), sights and sounds of the world around us (external stimuli). Our sensory apparatus helps us to convert this array of information into various sensations. The detection and subsequent interpretation of this information is the distinction between sensation and perception.

There are two main differences between sensation and perception:

1. **Duration:** Sensation is finite, meaning it has a limit or end. A smell will dissipate, a taste will fade. Perception, on the other hand, is infinite, meaning there is no limit to our perceptual process. We are constantly perceiving and assessing situations and events.

2. **Response:** Sensation is an immediate response to stimuli. Our nose responds directly to an odour without our consciously instructing it to do so. Perception will, however, always interpret stimuli. For example, our brain interprets the odour — as pleasant/

unpleasant — and we respond accordingly. Perception can also block out our awareness of certain stimuli.

As sensation is finite, sensory data received must have a beginning and an end: a threshold.

2.2.2 Thresholds

Our sensory receptors possess limitations. The term commonly used is 'threshold', referring to the boundary between what the senses can and cannot pick up. For example, dog whistles are below the human auditory threshold. A number of sensory thresholds exist but we are primarily interested in two: the absolute threshold and the differential threshold.

(a) **Absolute threshold:** This refers to the minimum stimulation necessary to be picked up by the human sensory receptors; the tickle of hair falling on your cheek or the pinprick of starlight just visible in a night sky. The absolute threshold is the lowest level at which an individual can experience a sensation.

(b) **Differential threshold:** This threshold, also known as either Weber's Law or Just Noticeable Difference (JND), refers to the minimal difference that can be detected between two stimuli. The JND is not an absolute or steady amount but is relative to the intensity of the original stimulus. For example, if an individual picks up a 1 lb bag of sugar in his right hand and then a 1 lb bag of flour in the other hand, he tends to compare the weight between the two. The conclusion: the weights are similar. If, at this point, 2 oz of sugar is added to the right hand (total 1 lb 2 oz), the individual would probably still perceive a similarity in the two weights. If, however, a further 2 oz is added to the right hand (totalling 1 lb 4 oz), the individual would *just notice a difference* between the two hands. A comparison of the left-hand weight with the right-hand weight (original stimulus) discerns a Just Noticeable Difference.

This JND occurs also in marketing and sales. The JND for customer awareness of sale prices is usually 20 per cent, all things being equal. In other words, a 20 per cent discount tends to be the just noticeable difference between the original price (original stimulus) and the sale price, and is sufficient for people to act upon. This is not to say, however, that companies or stores could not expend large sums of money bringing a 5 per cent price reduction to consumers' notice. The JND is often explained as an increase or decrease in a stimulus that can be reliably detected as a change in amount, value or intensity.

2.2.3 Habituation

This term is used when we stop attending to or noticing stimuli as they become familiar (Best, 1986). Our sensory apparatus no longer detects or attends to familiar stimuli; the ticking of a clock in a room is quite often not 'heard' because auditory receptors are acclimatised or habituated to the sound. If, however, the ticking ceases, quite often we 'miss' the noise and begin to focus on the silence. Likewise, parents are frequently habituated to their children's cries; visitors tend not to be. Many other examples spring to mind — the continuous shrill of a house alarm, the continuous appearance of 'sale' signs in shop windows. Habituation, while having obvious negative connotations, does serve a purpose in that it permits our sensory receptors simultaneously to 'deal' with familiar stimuli and yet accommodate fresh and novel aspects of our environment.

Although we can detect a multitude of stimuli, it is not physically possible to attend to them all. We therefore have to embark on what is known as a selection process: that is, selecting only stimuli which are both relevant and meaningful to us. This is referred to as perceptual selectivity.

2.3 PERCEPTUAL SELECTIVITY

2.3.1 Selection process

We are constantly bombarded with environmental stimuli. If we had no way of protecting ourselves it would be impossible to function effectively in such a world. We would become confused, mentally disorientated and unable to decide on how or when to act. Perceptual selectivity comes to our rescue. This is a process whereby individuals actively select relevant stimuli from their surroundings. Crossing a busy road requires perceptual selectivity. The list of stimuli vying for our attention, indeed bombarding our senses, is lengthy: other pedestrians, traffic lights, vehicles, advertising signs, noise levels, shops, passers-by, a mass of information about our environment. However, as our intended behaviour is to cross the road, we must, and do, select only those stimuli which will help us initiate and achieve our goal. These may be vehicles, traffic lights, pedestrians. Thus, we have perceptually selected relevant stimuli from the environment, screening out those not required.

Perceptual selectivity occurs in many everyday situations. When using the phone we focus on the voice at the other end and screen out distractions. At a party or a crowded bar, we screen out other people and focus on our partner's conversation. Within a marketing sphere, perceptual selectivity enables the consumer to focus on, say, a newly advertised product to the exclusion of competitors. For example, a fresh advertising campaign will gear itself to help the consumer perceptually to select its product by highlighting various features.

Selectivity may therefore be defined as a process through which we actively select stimuli, filtering or screening out information we do not need in order to prevent total bombardment of the senses. It is a process influenced by factors in the object being perceived (external) and factors in the person who is perceiving (internal). These factors, known as 'cues', may be divided into two interdependent categories and referred to as external and internal cues.

2.3.2 External cues

External cues affect perceptual selectivity because of their physical properties. The observed characteristics of the stimulus activate or trigger our senses, thus heightening our awareness of its existence. External cues consist of:

(a) **Size:** The larger the stimulus the more likely it is to capture the perceiver's attention. However, a small object may be used as a contrast against large objects. Whether large or small, size represents an important variable.

(b) **Intensity:** The brighter the lights or the louder the sounds, the better they capture attention. Television ads are always louder in volume than programmes so that viewers' attention will not wander during the commercial breaks.

(c) **Contrast:** Objects that contrast strongly with their backgrounds are more likely to be perceived than less contrasting objects. Safety regulations tend to be headed by the word 'DANGER' in capital letters and in a contrasting colour to the actual message.

(d) **Novelty:** This refers to a stimulus that appears unique or unexpected, often seen in a familiar setting. It is based on the premise that confounding the perceiver's expectations of normality will make him focus on anything that is unusual or 'not normal'. Advertising campaigns put this principle to good use with talking vegetables, dancing dishcloths.

(e) **Repetition:** The greater the number of times a message/word/ name is repeated, the more likely it is to be attended to (there is however a danger of habituation). Advertising uses this principle when brand-names and slogans are repeated at the beginning and end of ads. Repetition is almost a reinforcement mechanism.

(f) **Movement:** We automatically focus on objects that move. Our visual receptors, the eyes, follow — almost involuntarily — any type of movement. We become aware of the moving object against its surroundings, e.g. neon lights flashing, rotary display cabinets and moving window displays. Switzers, the Dublin department store, is famous nation-wide for its mobile Christmas window.

External cues serve the purpose of enhancing our awareness of stimuli by setting them apart from their surroundings. This works well but is frequently insufficient to retain our attention for more than a few moments. A second set of cues re-emphasises our awareness process; these are the internal cues.

2.3.3 Internal cues

Internal cues refer to the perceiver's personal factors, or internal variables, capable of influencing the extent to which he pays attention to a particular stimulus — that is, the feelings and experiences that affect the way a person observes.

These internal variables or cues include:

(a) **Past experiences:** These play a large role in our perception of the present situation. If an individual has suffered an unpleasant experience, say being bitten by a dog when a child, he may thereafter perceive dogs to be harmful creatures. It is the individual's experience, and therefore perception, that dogs are hurtful and not to be trusted. This is a very simplistic example but it demonstrates why people react differently, and sometimes surprisingly, to the same stimuli.

(b) **Response salience:** This refers to the tendency to focus on objects that relate to our immediate wants or match our interests. If we are particularly interested in environmental matters we will pick up information on the environment. We are remarkably sensitive to information (stimulus) that concerns a matter dear to us. Take a magazine photograph of a young girl sitting at a computer in her home. Two individuals will focus on different stimuli within the photograph. One individual interested in technology will focus on the type of software or technology used while the second perceiver, an avid home decorator, will focus on the surroundings of the child, especially colours or setting. Thus, what we need and what excites our interests are generally the factors that guide our sensory receptors.

(c) **Response disposition:** This refers to a tendency to recognise familiar objects more quickly than unfamiliar ones. Companies when advertising retain the colours of products or positioning of logos in an effort to aid the familiarisation process. A good example of this principle is McDonald's, the hamburger chain, with its distinctive yellow 'M'.

Although perceptual selectivity helps us select relevant stimuli, we still need to organise them in such a way as to make sense. Reading these words is, in itself, a perceptual organisational task. Perceptual selectivity has enabled us to focus on the printed matter (using size/contrast cues) but it is perceptual organisation that arranges the letters into words for us to interpret meaning.

2.4 PERCEPTUAL ORGANISATION

2.4.1 Organisation of stimuli

The name given to this patterning or organisation of stimuli is Gestalt — a German word literally translated as 'pattern'. 'Gestalt' originates from a German school of psychology's study of perception. It believed that individuals did not view stimuli as separate components but organised them into a recognisable whole or pattern, and by so doing extracted meaning.

Take, for example, the printed word

GESTALT

Perceptual selectivity enables us to select the lines but it requires perceptual organisation to give the lines meaning, i.e. letters. Gestalt takes it one step further by patterning the letters into one word — Gestalt — rather than leaving it as a string of separate letters. Likewise, if we refer to other people as 'good-looking', we are operationalising Gestalt. What we mean is that the person's eyes, skin, hair, mouth are all arranged in such a way as to be attractive, but rather than view the features as separate components, we organise them into a 'whole' view. The saying 'The whole is greater than the sum of its parts' encapsulates the principle of Gestalt.

Gestalt may be defined as a process through which incoming stimuli are organised or patterned in a systematic and meaningful way. It is a dynamic process depending on interpretation to yield understanding.

2.4.2 Laws of Gestalt

The Gestalt or organising (sometimes referred to as patterning) of stimuli is not a unitary process. Gestalt encompasses three basic laws or rules, each with an individual core concept and contributing towards overall meaning and ease of interpretation. These laws are:

(a) Figure-Ground
(b) Grouping
(c) Closure.

Law of figure-ground

While some aspects of a stimulus pattern appear to stand out as an object (figure), others provide a background (ground). The following diagram illustrates this point:

It is possible to interpret the stimulus as a vase (figure) against a black background (ground). Now alter your patterning of the stimuli, transforming the same picture into two dark profiles (figure) against a white background (ground). Similarly, the words on this page are 'figure' and the page itself is the ground. If you shift your patterning, the page becomes the figure and the writing the background. Shifting from one perception to another allows one to understand exactly what figure-ground organisation means.

The following figure is a well-known psychological portrait. Alter your perceptual patterning so you see alternately a young girl and an old woman.

Law of grouping

We perceive stimuli in groups rather than singularly; we can pick out one letter of a word but we tend to focus on the entire word. We group stimuli in order to enhance interpretation and meaning. This grouping rule encompasses three sub-laws.

(a) **Proximity:** Stimuli that are close together tend to be grouped together. The word 'deposed' appears in the following sentence:

FINDING WHO STOLE THE GARDEN
SPADE POSED A PROBLEM.

Because we group together words for ease of interpretation, we have to take time in trying to find the word. Once we have succeeded it is possible to locate the word quickly a second time.

(b) **Similarity:** Stimuli that are similar in size, shape, colour and form tend to be grouped together:

O O X O O

O O X O O

O O X O O

X X X X X X X

O O X O O

O O X O O

O O X O O

What we see is a selection of crosses and circles, yet on the basis of similarity we tend to focus on the crosses or the four groups of six circles.

(c) **Logic:** Stimuli are grouped according to what the mind perceives as logically organised. For example:

12

A   13   C

14

The interpretation of the middle figure depends on whether interpretation is horizontal or vertical. In the former, the figure is 'B', in the latter '13'. We impose logic on our perceptual process to facilitate understanding.

Law of closure

The mind has a tendency to complete a figure or shape in order to achieve overall consistent form.

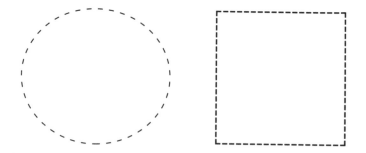

If asked to report what we see, we generally say a 'circle' or 'square'. However, in the true sense, what we actually see is a collection of dashes approximating a particular shape. Likewise,

IT IS N T VE Y H R TO EAD HIS EN ENCE.

We also have the ability to perform auditory closure tasks. That is, we can usually 'fill in' the gaps if we hear snippets of conversation in order to understand the discussion. We need hear only snatches of signature music to complete a tune or mentally 'close up' the programme. The signature tune will bring to mind the actual programme; we have closed up the tune and programme for ease of recognition. This is a technique commonly used in quiz shows.

Gestalt laws are the mind's attempt to place meaning and order on to stimuli. As humans we always try to make meaning out of what we perceive. More often than not, individuals are unaware of the effect Gestalt principles have on their perceptual processes. For example, we know that the law of auditory closure eases our interpretation of a half-heard conversation, yet most individuals do this subconsciously, unaware that a perceptual process is taking place. Most people do not realise that Gestalt laws are partly responsible for different interpretations of the same stimuli. How we use these laws again depends on the individual.

2.5 INDIVIDUAL'S PERCEPTUAL WORLD

2.5.1 Unique views

In 2.3 we discussed the selectivity of perception and why people notice some things and ignore others. Here we examine how two people who notice the same thing can put different meanings on what they see. Two people can watch the same film but 'see' different things. Why is this so?

2.5.2 Categorisation

Our perceptual learning builds up a set of personal mental categories to which our experiences are assigned and labelled. These perceptual categories are tremendously influential. Researchers Langer and Abelson (1974) showed a fifteen-minute video interview to a group of psychotherapists. The group was divided in two, with half being told the interviewee was applying for a job as a trainee psychotherapist, the other half that the interviewee was a mental patient. Those who had categorised the interviewee as an applicant perceived him as being realistic, sincere and pleasant. Those who categorised him as a mental patient perceived him as defensive and impulsive. In each case the psychotherapists utilised their mental categorisation systems, with the interviewee being labelled according to categorisation criteria. This example indicates clearly how powerful and influential our categorisations are. Frequently we are unaware that our categorisation system is operating and behave according to how we unconsciously interpret the situation.

2.5.3 Perceptual expectancies

Past experience, motives, context and suggestion all help to create a perceptual expectancy. We are set to perceive in a certain way and respond by seeing what we expect to see. Many perceptual expectancies are created by suggestion, as is demonstrated by the following two pieces of research.

(a) A psychology professor arranged an experiment in which a guest lecturer taught two of his classes. Beforehand one class was told that the lecturer was a 'rather cold person'; the other that he was a 'rather warm person'. After the lecture each group of students was interviewed. Students who received the 'cold' description perceived the lecturer as unhappy and irritable and did not participate in class. Those who received the 'warm' description saw the lecturer as happy and good-natured and did participate.

(b) A group of psychology students of the University of Oregon were asked to assess the facial expression of Kurt Waldheim (former President of Austria). Half were told he was in the Gestapo during the Second World War, responsible for horrific medical experiments on concentration camp inmates, and, not surprisingly, judged his expression to be cruel and frowning. Those students told he was a life-saving resistance hero judged his expression as warm and friendly (Rothbart and Birrell, 1977).

The implications of perceptual expectancies for the perceptual process are immense.

2.5.4 Selective perception

This process enables us to screen out information we do not wish to see or hear. It is similar to the general perceptual selectivity process but involves to a greater degree the internal aspects of the personality. For instance, psychologically we want to hear or believe only information that reaffirms our picture of the world. We do not want to focus on information that may be at odds with our beliefs or values. Consumers buying product 'seconds' will often screen out the damage or poor quality of the product in order to maintain the bargain's positive aspects. Individuals often select only those traits they wish to see in friends or acquaintances while ignoring the more negative aspects. The old cliché 'love is blind' in fact describes selective perception.

2.5.5 Perceptual defence

This process enables us to protect ourselves psychologically from threatening stimuli. Rather than face up to an unpleasant or menacing situation, we either select an alternative, or distort/ignore threatening stimuli. We operate our perceptual defence mechanisms when we feel we cannot cope with the reality of our present situation or when our long-held beliefs are challenged e.g. cigarette smokers will often gloss over the government warning printed on cigarette packets. It is important to note that perceptual defences may increase the difficulty of a situation because of the non-acceptance or distortion effected by the individual.

2.5.6 Attribution

The link between this process and perception is quite simple: people rarely perceive behaviour, they perceive behaviour which is caused. If people can interpret the cause or intention of behaviour, they feel they understand the situation better.

Kelley (1980) noted the existence of both internal and external attributions or causes. People determine the causes of behaviour both in themselves and in others by:

(a) **internal attribution:** behaviour is due to a person's own skill, ability or talent, e.g. Johnny is successful because he works very hard

(b) **external attribution:** behaviour is due to chance, ease of situation or aid given, e.g. Mark passed his driving test because the driving instructor was extremely lenient.

Three factors come into play when we attempt to 'read' causes in the behaviour we perceive: consensus, consistency and distinctiveness. Take, for example, two children in a classroom situation, both exhibiting loud behaviour. The teacher perceives Claire in a far more negative light than Conor. Why? The teacher's attribution process is at work. She is assigning causes to each child's behaviour — remember we do not perceive behaviour as much as behaviour which is caused. The teacher assigns an internal, almost deliberately negative cause to Claire, i.e. Claire is being rowdy because she enjoys being disruptive, while Conor is assigned an external cause, i.e. Conor is being rowdy because the rest of the class is also being noisy. Claire is deliberately annoying while Conor is being influenced by others. How is this attribution arrived at? The teacher is using the three attribution factors:

consensus: the extent to which a group member is acting in accordance with the group

consistency: the extent to which the observed person behaves consistently in this particular situation, and in other similar situations
distinctiveness: the extent to which the observed individual behaves differently when faced with different situations.

Returning to Claire and Conor:

— Claire is rowdy, regardless of her companions' behaviour. She is always rowdy in this teacher's class. In fact, she is rowdy in every situation, whether in class, at home or in the playground.

— Conor is rowdy because the whole class is rowdy. His behaviour tends to be influenced by the general class behaviour. He is not usually disruptive in any other area of life, whether at play or at home.

Attribution theory has important implications in an organisational setting. Where management attributes poor performance levels to internal causes, e.g. Daniel is not performing well because he is not motivated, employee–management relationships may suffer. It may well be the case that Daniel is performing poorly merely because he does not experience adequate resource back-up.

It is interesting to note that when we make attributions regarding ourselves, we claim internal attributions for positive results, e.g. I won the lottery because I picked my family's birthdays for numbers, and external attributions for negative outcomes, e.g. I didn't win because the numbers were all low and therefore unusual.

We have seen that an individual's perceptual world is far from simple. There are many interrelating variables influencing our view of our world. If the process of viewing the environment is fraught with difficulties, is the process of viewing other people also complex? We now examine what is involved when all the components of the perceptual process are targeting another individual, i.e. social perception.

2.6 SOCIAL PERCEPTION

2.6.1 Views of others

Social perception is an important part of the perceptual process. It is how we perceive or 'see' other people. As we have learned, perception is an individual and complex process even when we are viewing events or situations not directly affecting us. Think how much more prone to errors our 'people' perception must be. Inaccurate perception has important consequences. In the workplace, misperceptions of attitudes and motivations can have severe workforce repercussions. In the marketing world, consumer misconceptions of a marketing campaign may cause brand failure. In real life, misperceptions of other people may cause us to miss out on friendships or to 'label' people incorrectly.

How then do we perceive people? What cues do we focus on? What do we selectively screen out? What errors do we make? There are three basic interactive influences affecting our perceptions of others:

(a) characteristics of the person perceived

(b) characteristics of the perceiver

(c) characteristics of the situation.

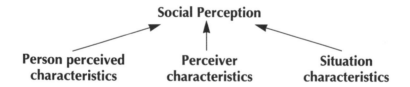

Social Perception

Person perceived characteristics   **Perceiver characteristics**   **Situation characteristics**

2.6.2 Characteristics of person perceived

We tend to perceive and form impressions of other people on two levels: one consciously taking in their unique set of personal characteristics, the other unconsciously absorbing and interpreting according to our categorisation system. Specific influences on our interpretations include:

(a) **Physical appearance:** This includes age, gender, height, weight and dress. For example, the concept of power-dressing, begun in the United States, quickly spread world-wide. People wearing business suits signal status and professionalism. We expect and feel secure when we see doctors dressed in white coats, hence the rash of television ads denoting 'professionals' for toothpaste, household bleach and petrol. Uniforms in general signal efficiency, expertise and responsibility.

(b) **Verbal communication:** This covers accents, tones of voices, articulateness. Accents can give geographical, social and educational cues. Witness 'soap operas' depicting characters from a specific social class. Tone or pitch of voice offers perceptions of personality types; high pitch can indicate a certain 'nervousness' while a more evenly modulated tone offers an impression of confidence. Choice and use of words also contribute to social perception.

(c) **Non-verbal communication:** Body language is unconsciously transmitted through various channels, i.e. face, eyes, posture. We subconsciously pick up and respond to these signals, thus creating a sub-level of communication. Avoiding eye contact is considered bad manners, giving the impression of non-attention; continuous posture-shifting denotes psychological unease; and spatial considerations imply relationship difference, e.g. the space between employee and boss is always much wider than the space between two friends.

(d) **Ascribed attributes:** We tend to perceive people according to their ascribed attributes, e.g. status, occupation. The higher the status the more we see the person as capable and self-assured. Likewise, professions seem to evoke more esteem than, say, administrative jobs. In each case the person is being judged not for himself but for his ascribed attributes. Frequently we hear the complaint from media celebrities that people respond to them not as mortals but as stars, an ascribed attribute.

2.6.3 Characteristics of perceiver

Characteristics or make-up of the perceiver (the person doing the looking) also play an important role in person perception. Many of these characteristics are similar to internal cues examined in 'Perceptual Selectivity' above and can greatly influence the way we look and feel towards another person. These include:

(a) **Self-concept:** refers to the picture we have of ourselves. If we accurately understand ourselves, we tend accurately to perceive other people. Research indicates that the more accepting we are of ourselves, the more accepting and less threatened we are as regards other people (Steers, 1991).

(b) **Cognitive structure:** refers to our ability to perceive others based on multiple criteria. The more we can differentiate between people using a selection of variables and characteristics, e.g. pleasant, hard-working and reliable, the more accurate our perception will be.

(c) **Previous experience with the individual:** refers to the influence of earlier experience on our perception. An unpleasant incident involving a particular individual in the past will cause us to categorise or label that person negatively. We find it very difficult to alter our opinion of them at any future time even though evidence may be presented to this effect. It is hard to rid ourselves of this first impression.

2.6.4 Characteristics of situation

Two situational influences affect our social perception — location (where the initial meeting took place and under what conditions) and company (the people with whom we are observed).

(a) **Location:** Whether the location or surroundings are formal or informal can alter a person's perception. Meeting someone for the first time in a formal situation, e.g. an interview, can give a certain impression; meeting them later in a less formal setting, e.g. a party, causes us a certain amount of confusion. It is extremely difficult to 'switch' perceptions once we have 'tied' people to a particular setting. It is rather like failing to recognise a work colleague in a social setting.

(b) **Company:** The people we are observed with often have a part to play in another's perception of us. Individuals tend to group or label others for ease of identification and we often categorise a person by the company he keeps. This in itself is not a fault as long as we do not err in our judgments.

2.6.5 Influencing factors

Individual differences account for a tremendous amount of subjectivity and unreliability in perception. This is particularly true in relation to person perception, when the process of perception is influenced, or biased, by a number of factors, namely:

◆   halo effect
◆   stereotyping
◆   projection
◆   personality beliefs
◆   first impressions
◆   attribution bias.

(a) **Halo effect:** A judgment or perception of a person is often made on the basis of one characteristic, e.g. politeness. We tend then to attribute to that person other similar and logical (to us) characteristics such as honesty, cheerfulness and reliability. We do not know if these other characteristics exist within the person observed, but we believe so purely on the basis of the one observed characteristic.

(b) **Stereotyping:** We tend to judge people according to the group to which we feel or perceive they belong. We have a tendency to want to categorise or label people so that we can 'place' them in our minds and attribute to them a set of expected characteristics. So instead of dealing with people on an individual level, we frequently stereotype them as representatives of a particular group or class. This act of stereotyping can in fact be useful. It reduces ambiguity, enables us to classify people quickly and simplifies our interpersonal world. However, it can also lead to misperception and loss of individuality on the part of the perceived. Stereotyping is done in a vast number of ways, including:

nationality	we often classify nations, e.g. Americans are loud, Germans are serious, Irish are happy-go-lucky
age	older workers are less able to change than a young workforce
gender	men make better leaders than women; women make better home-makers than men.

(c) **Projection:** This occurs when we attribute to others characteristics or feelings that we ourselves experience. We frequently make inferences about the causes of people's behaviour based purely on what we would do or feel in a similar situation.

(d) **Personality beliefs:** This refers to the 'implicit personality theory' we all possess. That is, we use limited information about a person for generalisation purposes. We believe that certain personality traits 'go with' others: jolly and fat; hard-working and honest; talkative and extroverted. Because of this implicit personality theory, we tend largely to 'create' an image or perception of a person.

(e) **First impressions:** These tend to be long-lasting and difficult to contradict. First impressions trigger our perceptual set, thus we see a person in a particular way that has already been decided upon. Webster

(1982) indicates that unskilled interviewers make tentative first impressions or judgments about interviewees within the first four minutes of the interview, and spend the remaining interview time selecting information that conforms with, and confirms, these first impressions.

(f) **Attribution bias:** As we know from 2.5.6, attribution theory deals with the allocating of reasons for people's behaviour — on either an internal or an external basis. Attribution is, however, vulnerable to the following errors:

(i) **intention:** an act seen as motivated by gain tends to be viewed in a less positive light (external attribution) than an act which is perceived as unselfish or having no ulterior motive (internal attribution). If, say, a celebrity advertises sports shoes and it is disclosed he is a director of the manufacturing company, then the credibility of both celebrity and product is viewed differently by the consumer. The prevailing consumer attribute may well be, 'They are only doing it for the money.'

(ii) **status:** the status of a person we perceive affects how we attribute causes to their behaviour. The higher the status, the more responsible for their actions the person is perceived to be.

(iii) **self-serving bias:** when anything positive happens to us, we tend to attribute internal causation (e.g. I set the wheels in motion) while to anything negative we attribute external causation (e.g. if the time had been right the business would have succeeded). Curiously, we tend to do the opposite when attributing causes of other people's behaviour. It is common practice for management to attribute an employee's non-performance or failure to his own efforts (internal attribution) rather than to the actual work situation or the employee's supervisors (external attribution).

The foregoing demonstrates the complexity of social perception. Far from making simple judgments about a person or their actions, we unconsciously engage in many processes that may or may not give accurate results. We must at all times be aware of such influences.

This chapter has examined the human perceptual process and its ability to make sense of the individual's environment. If we are to understand why people behave as they do, we must first understand how they view the world. Each person possesses his own perceptual world; whether or not it is an accurate portrayal, it is his view of the world.

2.7 SUMMARY

1. Perception is a process whereby individuals select, organise and interpret stimuli in order to give meaning to their environment.
2. Sensory receptors receive incoming stimuli in the form of sensations but do not interpret them.
3. Perceptual selectivity is the process whereby individuals actively select and screen out stimuli to prevent bombardment of the senses. This is influenced by external and internal cues.
4. Perceptual organisation — Gestalt — enables us to organise stimuli into a meaningful picture of the world.
5. An individual's perceptual world consists of many variables, including categorisation, expectancies, selective perception, perceptual defence, attributions.
6. Person perception involves three variables: perceived, perceiver and situation, and is influenced by many factors, such as halo effect, stereotyping, projection, attribution bias.

2.8 EXAM QUESTIONS

1. Discuss the ways in which sensation differs from perception.
2. Indicate how the physical properties of stimuli are important in gaining people's attention. (MII, 1991)
3. What is perceptual organisation?
4. Examine the variables and errors involved in the person's perceptual process. (MII, 1991)
5. Examine some of the problems in social perception.

Learning and Memory

3.1 INTRODUCTION

3.2 BEHAVIOURIST LEARNING THEORIES
3.2.1 Classical conditioning
3.2.2 Operant conditioning
3.2.3 Evaluation

3.3 COGNITIVE LEARNING THEORIES
3.3.1 Insight learning
3.3.2 Latent learning
3.3.3 Evaluation
3.3.4 Comparison — Behaviourist and
Cognitive theories

3.4 MEMORY
3.4.1 Functions of memory
3.4.2 Atkinson and Shiffrin model of memory
3.4.3 Memory and forgetting

3.5 SUMMARY

3.6 EXAM QUESTIONS

Learning Objectives

After studying this chapter you should be able to:

— *Understand what learning is*
— *Describe and explain the Behaviourist School of learning*
— *Describe and explain the Cognitive School of learning*
— *Identify the differences between the Behaviourist and Cognitive approaches*
— *Be familiar with the stages of memory and understand some of the reasons why we forget.*

3.1 INTRODUCTION

It seems self-evident that we as human beings have the ability to learn many things: to walk and talk, to develop relationships and to acquire new skills. Although it may appear that this 'just happens' and is integral to our humanity, it is in fact part of the learning process.

In a later chapter we investigate how individuals learn to live in society, to adopt approved behavioural roles and harmonise within their culture. However, at present we are concerned with how individuals learn responses, behaviours and skills. Many theories offer themselves as frameworks for the study of learning behaviour and we examine some in this chapter.

Why are we interested in learning? From an organisational perspective we hope to understand how best to teach employees to behave in accordance with organisational principles. This includes areas such as training, performance levels, motivation and, most importantly, establishes a clear work–reward learning relationship. From a marketing perspective, we hope to be able to 'teach' consumers to purchase, or at least attempt to shape their buying behaviour. The more advertising agencies discover how a consumer learns the better able they are to develop their campaigns. From a real-life perspective we understand that learning or the ability to learn links us to our world. If we could not learn we would be immediately set apart from our peers. We teach children basic tasks; we teach animals basic tricks; and we teach ourselves basic skills. The concept of learning is inherent in humanity.

We examine first the Behaviourist School of learning, i.e. the conditioning approach to learning, and then the Cognitive School, i.e. the information-processing approach. These two schools tend to be viewed as mutually exclusive, yet have certain areas of agreement. We evaluate both models.

The final section in this chapter includes a model of memory. We look at how people remember, how they retrieve stored information and under what circumstances they forget. It would seem obvious to most people that learning must involve the memory system. We hope to present a clear and unambiguous model of memory that contributes to our task of understanding human behaviour.

In studying learning, we first offer a definition in order to ground the concept: 'Learning may be defined as a relatively permanent change in behaviour occurring as a result of experience or practice' (Coon, 1986).

3.2 BEHAVIOURIST LEARNING THEORIES

The Behaviourist School (sometimes referred to as the Connectionist School) has four major proponents, each contributing to the Behaviourist model:

(i)   Ivan Pavlov

(ii) John Watson

(iii) E.L. Thorndike

(iv) B.F. Skinner.

Each considered learning a process of constant conditioning, constant association and constant reinforcing. They believed in the concept of learning laws, applicable to all, regardless of environmental or social variables. We concentrate on two: Ivan Pavlov and Classical conditioning, and B.F. Skinner and Operant conditioning.

3.2.1 Classical conditioning

Ivan Pavlov (1849–1936), a Russian physiologist, believed in the concept of **association**, and he considered it the only way learning would occur. Pavlov's Classical conditioning is built upon respondent behaviour: that is, reflexes which are directly elicited by certain stimuli.

Pavlov used as the basis for conditioning the reflexive salivary response of a dog to the smell of food. He believed he could link, or associate, the stimulus (food) which elicited the reflexive response (salivation) to another stimulus which would in turn elicit the same response. To prove it he attempted to link the smell of food with the sound of a bell, so that the dogs would then salivate to the sound of the bell, without the food being presented. In other words, Pavlov hoped to 'teach' a dog to salivate to the sound of a bell.

Within the experiment Pavlov utilised four variables:

i) **unconditioned stimulus** — natural or unlearned stimulus

ii) **unconditioned response** — natural or unlearned response

iii) **conditioned stimulus** — stimulus that acquires the ability to elicit a response after being associated with an unconditioned stimulus

iv) **conditioned response** — learned response that follows an unconditioned stimulus and conditioned stimulus pairing.

Pavlov observed that when he gave the dogs in his laboratory pieces of meat (**unconditioned stimulus**) they would salivate (**unconditioned response**), as is natural since salivation aids digestion. The meat was obviously the stimulus as it evoked the response of salivation within the dogs. Both were unconditioned in the sense that the dogs did not have to be trained to respond in such a manner.

Pavlov set out to match the unconditioned response (UCR) to a conditioned stimulus (CS). In this case, Pavlov wanted to see if he could make the dogs salivate (**conditioned response**, as it would now be) when he presented them with the sound of a bell (**conditioned stimulus**) (Pavlov, 1927). His method involved:

Stage 1: Presenting the dogs with a piece of meat (unconditioned stimulus) and observing them salivate (unconditioned response).

Stage 2: Presenting the dogs with a piece of meat (unconditioned stimulus) and ringing a bell at the same time (conditioned stimulus), and then observing them salivate. This was repeated until the dogs were familiar with the sound of the bell. Note that Pavlov was trying to *pair*, or associate, the sound of the bell with the meat in order for the former to gain the power of the unconditioned stimulus.

Stage 3: Ringing the bell (conditioned stimulus) and observing the dogs salivate (conditioned response).

Pavlov succeeded — he conditioned the dogs to associate the sound of the bell with the meat, and was able to bring about a salivation response. Pavlov's Classical conditioning may be defined as when 'a previously neutral stimulus begins to elicit a response through *association* with a paired stimulus' (Pavlov, 1927). The dogs eventually associated the bell and food with one another, thus Pavlov succeeded in teaching them a behaviour through conditioning.

The same phenomenon occurs when, for example, someone in our family says, 'Tea's ready.' When we hear this phrase, though we may have neither smelt nor tasted the food, we will probably start salivating. In this case, the conditioned stimulus is the phrase 'Tea's ready' and the conditioned response is the salivation.

A number of Pavlovian concepts were drawn from the above:

(a) **Stimulus generalisation** is the effect generated by one stimulus which can be transposed onto another, similar, stimulus. For example, Pavlov discovered that if he sounded a buzzer the dogs found it sufficiently like the bell for it to evoke the same response, i.e. salivation. So, when we are in a friend's house we are still conditioned by an instinct to answer the door even though the doorbell may not sound exactly like our own. In this case, we are generalising the knowledge of the sound of our own doorbell to that of the different house we are in.

(b) **Extinction** occurs when we remove an important part of the stimulus-response mechanism. Pavlov stated that if an important stimulus were removed for a sufficiently long period, the conditioned response would eventually disappear. During his experiments, he discovered that if he presented the bell for a number of trials without the meat, the salivation response disappeared, or became 'extinct'. Thus, a conditioned response (salivation) will not last indefinitely unless reinforced by the unconditioned stimulus (meat). The same effect occurs when a manufacturer advertises a 'free' offer, which turns out to be nothing of the sort. After the consumer purchases the product a few times without reward, the effect will become extinct and he will cease to believe the manufacturer's claims.

(c) **Spontaneous recovery:** Once the effect of the conditioned stimulus (the bell) has been extinguished we can re-present the unconditioned stimulus (the meat, in this case) along with the bell and it will once again become effective. This process is known as 'spontaneous recovery'. Pavlov discovered that the dogs began to salivate when he re-presented the meat after an absence. This can also happen in the world of marketing when a producer reintroduces special offers which had initially induced customers to buy the product.

(d) **Higher order conditioning** is the transposition of one conditioned stimulus to another. Pavlov discovered that if he presented a card showing a black dot simultaneously with a bell sounding, the dogs would begin the association process and salivate at the sight of the card. He termed this **higher order conditioning**. It differs from stimulus generalisation in that the bell and the buzzer are presented separately in stimulus generalisation, whereas the bell and card are presented together in higher order conditioning. Advertisers aim for a similar effect when they attempt to associate a number of desirable images with their product.

Both Pavlov and Skinner understood human learning in terms of stimulus-response (S-R) bonds, and it is to Skinner's model of learning that we now turn.

3.2.2 Operant conditioning

B.F. Skinner (1904–1990) is one of the most important psychologists of the twentieth century. He took Pavlov's work further and developed it to such an extent that his own findings have proved useful in situations as disparate as acknowledging and enhancing employee performance in the workplace and shaping social behaviour in mental hospitals. There are few areas in which his theories have not been applied. His theories offer an accurate description of the ways in which we learn and are capable of adjusting our behaviour in changing circumstances (Skinner, 1953). Basically, Operant conditioning may be defined as when 'an individual operates on, or is instrumental in, the environment to produce a change that leads to a reward'. The key factor for Skinner is reinforcement. A number of Skinnerian concepts were drawn from the above principles:

(a) **Positive and negative reinforcement:** Skinner introduced this notion, demonstrating it by means of responses from rats in what became known as a **Skinner box**. For example, when a rat touched a lever in the box it was rewarded by food. Skinner declared the behaviour had been positively reinforced (and thus learned), and that a simple stimulus (rat touching the lever) response (rat receives food) bond was in operation. When we buy a product and receive a money-off voucher we are being positively reinforced, and are more likely to repeat our actions to gain another voucher. Manufacturers have 'taught' us to buy their products.

If, however, the rat had touched the lever and received a slight electric shock, Skinner would declare that the behaviour had been negatively reinforced and was unlikely to be repeated. According to Skinner, the rat had *learned* not to press the lever. An everyday example of negative reinforcement is children receiving a slap for not tidying away their toys. This negative reinforcement may continue until the children realise that in order to avoid the slap they have to tidy the toys.

The importance of the notion of positive and negative reinforcement lies in the ability of the person (or animals) concerned to elicit a positive or negative response from those who supply the reinforcement. In other words, in Skinner's analysis of learning, his subjects were able to influence their environment through recognising and responding to reinforcement techniques. Pavlov's subjects were passive while Skinner's played an active part in their behavioural consequences.

(b) **Selective reinforcement and discriminative stimulus:** Skinner also introduced these concepts. For example, he tried selectively reinforcing his rats' behaviour by rewarding the pressing of the lever only when a light shone. The rat learned to press the lever only when there was a continuous light — the light serving as the discriminative stimulus.

'Happy hours' in pubs operate on the same principle, rewarding customers for drinking during particular times by offering cheaper drinks.

(c) **Partial and continuous reinforcement:** The former refers to random rewarding of the subject and the latter to continuous rewarding of the subject for his actions. For example, partial reinforcement would occur if the rat in Skinner's Box were rewarded for five out of ten lever presses. Continuous reinforcement would occur if the rat were rewarded for each press. Skinner noted that behaviour partially reinforced lasted longer as the rats tended to repeat their actions in the expectation of a reward.

Partial reinforcement is often used in marketing by rewarding consumers with a prize (of a holiday, say) in return for buying a certain amount of a particular product, rather than each time they purchase it. Random partial reinforcement is often used by the cola companies when they etch letters on a certain quantity of their cans, leading to the purchaser's receiving a prize. Partial negative reinforcement is used when a basketball player has to leave the field for accumulating a certain number of 'fouls', whereas in football, players who foul are more likely to receive continuous negative reinforcement by being booked or sent off each time they commit an offence.

(d) **Passive and active avoidance:** In passive avoidance we avoid an aversive stimulus by not responding, e.g. a child may refrain from fighting if he knows he will be punished. In active avoidance a child would actively avoid a situation involving fighting in order to avoid negative reinforcement (punishment).

(e) **Primary and secondary reinforcement:** Skinner differentiated between primary and secondary reinforcers. Primary reinforcers are basic reinforcers usually fulfilling a physiological need — food, heat or light. When a rat receives food for pressing a lever it primarily seeks the food, thus reinforcing its behaviour. Secondary reinforcers, on the other hand, are learned reinforcers, usually from the learning environment. For example, a child might associate its high chair (secondary reinforcer) with being fed (food as the primary reinforcer).

3.2.3 Evaluation

The Behaviourist approach to learning has had a world-wide influence. We can see simple everyday stimulus-response learning behaviours all around us. How many times have we tried to screw off the cap of a bottle only to find that it is a flip top? How many times have we tried to push a door open only to find we have to pull it towards us? In each case we have been conditioned one way and continue to apply our learning, not realising that such behaviour is inappropriate.

Many learning theorists (Coon, 1986), although accepting the great contributions of Pavlov and Skinner, have criticised the Behaviourist model as a whole. The grounds for these criticisms include:

(a) **ignoring human ability to learn.** The Behaviourist model excludes our ability to go beyond the situation and have independent and complex thoughts. It believes learning is rooted in conditioning.

(b) **ignoring learner influence.** People differ in motivations, attitudes and emotions. The Behaviourist approach disregards these variables not only between individuals but also within people. For example, one day an individual's motivation may be high, therefore learning will occur. The following day the same individual may possess little or no motivation; hence, regardless of the situation, the subject will not learn.

(c) **dismisses individual differences.** Individuals' learning ability involves many variables, such as perceptions, past experiences, interests and motivations. Constant conditioning does not nullify them.

(d) **learning tends not to persist in absence of reinforcement.** If rewards cease, it is more than likely that behavioural responses (and therefore learning) also cease.

Behaviourist models are important within the framework of learning theories and have many different applications. Their main opposition comes from an approach which analyses what happens within the 'head' rather than the reflexive behaviour of the subject. This is the Cognitive School of learning.

3.3 COGNITIVE LEARNING THEORIES

There are two main branches within the Cognitive approach to learning: the **Insight** approach and the **Latent** approach. Superficially, they seem to have little in common, but the following descriptions show that they are alike in positing an organising principle which helps us to learn. While the Connectionist School talked of S-R bonds, the Cognitive theorists developed this to read 'S-O-R' bonds, through the use of an organising principle ('O'). The Cognitive theorists believe that learning involves higher mental processes and take an almost information-processing, or problem-solving, approach. We examine two models, Insight learning and Latent learning.

3.3.1 Insight learning

Wolfgang Kohler, a member of the Gestalt School of psychology, believed that the basis of learning was understanding the arrangement of the constituent parts of a situation. Further, that for learning truly to have taken place it was necessary to show that the skill/act/knowledge learned was both repeatable and generalisable.

Kohler tried to discover whether apes could arrive at the solution to a problem according to the Gestalt principles already cited. He set the apes a problem: how to reach a bunch of bananas suspended from the top of their cage, inaccessible by climbing. Kohler provided the components of the solution by placing certain objects — boxes, chairs and sticks — at various locations in the cage. Technically, the apes could solve the problem if they managed to use each of the component parts of the solution (the boxes, the chairs and the sticks) *together*. After a number of unsuccessful attempts to reach the bananas by jumping or using the props individually, the chimps seemed to rest and contemplate.

Kohler posited that they could reach a solution if they could perceive the various composites of the problem within the same perceptual field. Ultimately they were indeed able to use each of the props together and solve the problem. Kohler observed the apes achieving the solution in a 'eureka' manner; that is, they had been puzzling out the solution for some time, but the answer came in a sudden burst of insight. In the same way, we may be trying to solve an anagram puzzle for a number of hours and all at once realise the answer — like the originator of the 'eureka' phrase, Archimedes, who solved a problem as his bath overflowed.

3.3.2 Latent learning

Latent learning, postulated by Edward C. Tolman, advances the idea that there is latent (or hidden) within us the ability to solve certain problems, though this may not be readily apparent in the learning situation.

Tolman based his theory on the outcome of experiments with rats. Essentially, Tolman placed rats in a maze to test their ability to learn the quickest way out. He split his test group in two and rewarded only one group with food on reaching the exit. He varied the solution to the problem, introducing obstacles into the maze, still differentiating between the two groups on the basis of reward. He found as time passed that the reward group was faster to find the solution to the problem. However, after ten trials he began to reward the second group in an effort to see if it would be able to find its way out as quickly as the group which had initially been rewarded. His hypothesis was supported. The second group now became as fast as the reward group in its ability to learn their way out of the maze. Tolman suggested that, despite its being rewarded only ⅔ times, the ability to learn had been latent in the non-reward group, with the reward triggering learning. So during non-reward time the second group had actually been building up cognitive maps or internal representations of the maze (learning the layout) and, when necessary, could display the learning, and be rewarded. Tolman said that individuals possess the ability to learn many skills if the right stimulus is presented in order to elicit those skills.

3.3.3 Evaluation

Both cognitive models examined here embrace the notion of an organising principle mediating the learning process. The Cognitive School sees learning as very much an individual process, influenced by such variables as motivation, perception and feedback.

Cognitive theorists agree that memory has an important role in a learning situation, in that it aids the process of thinking, storing and retrieving information. The main aspect of the Cognitive School's theories of learning is the idea that an 'organising', or reflective, principle is at work when we learn; therefore we do not simply respond to stimuli.

3.3.4 Comparison — Behaviourist and Cognitive theories

(a) **Stimulus-Response versus Stimulus-Organisation-Response:**
Pavlov states that learning is just a conditioning of responses and
Skinner suggests that learning is only the result of reinforcement. In
other words, they are saying that memory is simply acquiring
'Stimulus-Response' bonds which can then be applied in particular
situations. Kohler and Tolman believe that a person does not merely
respond to a stimulus, and so learn, but actively organises the
learning situation in order to process the stimuli, and so learns. Thus
'Stimulus-Organisation-Response' bonds are acquired.

(b) **The role of memory:** Memory is an important part of the learning
process for Tolman, as it helped the rats in his experiment to learn
the correct route when a reward was presented. For Pavlov, learning
is merely the reflexive storage of facts, and experiences play no role.

(c) **Individual differences:** The Cognitive School considers learning
an individual process influenced by variables such as motivation,
perception and feedback. The Behaviourists would refute this, and
say that we all learn in the same manner, irrespective of individual
differences.

3.4 MEMORY

Memory is an active system that receives, stores, organises, alters
and recovers information.

3.4.1 Functions of memory

Memory has many uses in our lives. Although it is considered a
hypothetical construct, it has multiple functions:

(a) **It records** — provides a storage facility, ranging from specific
personal episodes in our lives to the more general knowledge
function providing a knowledge base from which we view our life
situation and that of the world around us.

(b) **It organises and updates** — arranges and rearranges our
information, knowledge and feelings into compatible user states.

(c) **It learns** — provides us with building-blocks so that we can increase our knowledge.

(d) **It operates in the world** — makes memories, recollections, learning experiences accessible when required.

In order to remember something, a person must be able to:

(a) **encode** — accept information in a usable form. Information we wish to commit to memory must be entered in terms we understand, similar to a computer program. Unless we use the correct inputting program a computer will refuse to accept the information. In our case badly entered information will not be remembered correctly.

(b) **store** — be able to hold information in a certain fashion — we tend to store in line with our personal categorisation or reference system. For example, behavioural science information is stored in our memory apart from any other topic.

(c) **retrieve** — ability to recover information. This function is achieved only if the previous two stages are completed correctly, i.e. information is entered in an understandable way and organised into specific categories.

Remembering is a complex phenomenon, widely studied by psychologists, yet questions concerning why we remember, how we remember and why we forget are still posed by laypeople and psychologists alike.

In order for us to attempt to understand this phenomenon and offer tentative explanations of its workings, we must first address the question: 'What is memory?' A general definition could be: 'the receiving, storing and retrieving of all types of sensory information'.

Many models of memory exist. We examine that of Atkinson and Shiffrin (1971).

3.4.2 Atkinson and Shiffrin model of memory

Atkinson and Shiffrin proposed a multi-store model of memory with three compartments working in harmony. Basically, information is received through the **Sensory Memory** and if we wish to retain the image/sound we pass it into the **Short-Term Memory**, which in turn transfers the relevant information into the **Long-Term Memory**, where it is stored for later use. The following diagram provides a simple model. We describe the actions in each compartment in point form.

Incoming Information → Sensory/Perceptual memory → Short-term memory → Long-term memory

Sensory Memory

(a) receives incoming information from the environment.

(b) holds an exact copy of what is seen or heard for up to two seconds.

(c) iconic (visual) memory lasts for approximately half a second.

(d) echoic (auditory) memory lasts for up to two seconds.

(e) holds information sufficiently long to facilitate transfer to the second compartment, i.e. Short-Term Memory.

Short-Term Memory

(a) also referred to as working memory.

(b) conscious process in that we deliberately attempt to memorise.

(c) temporary storehouse containing only information that has been purposely selected.

(d) needs rehearsal for retention. For example, if we are asked to remember a telephone number, we tend to keep repeating the digits until (i) we can write it down, or (ii) it has been transferred into Long-Term Memory.

(e) possesses a limited storage/duration capacity. Storage tends to be limited to 7±2 units of information, i.e. 5 and 9 units are the minimum and maximum storage limits. The limit of the duration capacity of Short-Term Memory is fifteen to thirty seconds.

(f) 'Chunking' occurs in Short-Term Memory (Millar, 1956). We 'chunk' together items in an effort to make more space. For example, if you were asked to remember the following twelve words: *dog, brown, tall, man, fence, lead, jump, the, his, took, to, above*, rather than individually remembering the words, which in turn would fill up the Short-Term Memory, a far better method is to make a sentence out of them, thus converting the twelve units into one. Another chunking strategy is to 'pair' up words, again working on the 'freeing up' method.

Long-Term Memory

(a) information is transferred from Short-Term Memory only if it is meaningful and makes sense.

(b) limitless capacity and duration. For example, we retain and accumulate memories from early childhood throughout our life.

(c) tends to be an unconscious process (except for deliberate learning experiences), and rather complex. We are never quite sure why we remember a certain person's face, or a particular incident.

(d) memories for iconic, echoic and motor movements reside here.

(e) often regarded as a permanent storehouse of memories.

3.4.3 Memory and forgetting

The study of forgetting has helped researchers to understand the nature of memory. If we know some of the reasons that memory does not operate successfully, we can deduce parts of its structure. The following are some suggested reasons that we forget:

(a) **Retroactive inhibition:** Learning a new piece of information may interfere with previously held information on the same subject. Thus when a manufacturer brings out a new brand of washing powder it may retroactively inhibit our memory of the older brand.

(b) **Proactive inhibition:** This is the opposite: namely, where previously held information inhibits retention of new information. For example, a friend's new telephone number might not be remembered because we were so used to the old number. Thus the old number proactively inhibits the newer number.

(c) **Emotional factors:** If an individual is upset, memory for detail is poor. Courts, for example, are loath to convict solely on the basis of a victim's testimony — even though this may be the only evidence available. This is because the emotions of the time can interfere with the encoding process, hence accuracy of recall.

Improving memory

A number of strategies exist to improve memory, each placing strong emphasis on properly encoding information so that it can be effectively retrieved:

(a) **Mnemonics:** Device to aid memory, such as combinations of letters which stand for the first letters of a number of other words and ideas, minimising the amount of information and thus making it easier to learn. For example, if we were to try to learn the colours of the rainbow we could construct the mnemonic **BOY GIVR**, which stands for:

Blue	**G**reen
Orange	**I**ndigo
Yellow	**V**iolet
	Red

The most commonly used memory aids in relation to the colours of the spectrum are 'Richard Of York Gave Battle In Vain' and 'Ring Out Your Great Bells In Victory'.

(b) **Regular rehearsal:** If we rehearse information regularly, we are more likely to remember. Most of us have little problem remembering our own phone number because we rehearse it so often. Researchers have shown that over 50 per cent of material which is not rehearsed is lost the next day.

(c) **Dependent learning:** Material is learned more effectively if it is retrieved in a similar situation to that in which it was learned, e.g. doing an examination in a quiet room should simulate the quiet conditions in which the study was done. Thus retrieval is dependent on the learning context.

This chapter has investigated an individual's learning behaviour. We have identified a wide range of learning situations and the conditions that govern learning behaviour. We have, for example, shown that learning theorists do not speak with one voice about the role of incentives, rewards or punishments, and that there is much disagreement on the importance and practice of understanding and insight in the learning process. Nevertheless, despite differences, the various approaches provide the reader with an overall view of an individual's learning environment.

3.5 SUMMARY

1. The two main theories of learning are the Behaviourist approach and the Cognitive approach.
2. The Behaviourist approach consists of Classical conditioning (Pavlov), emphasising the role of association in learning, and Operant conditioning (Skinner), emphasising the importance of positive and negative reinforcement.
3. The Cognitive approach to learning consists of the Insight and the Latent (Tolman) approaches.
4. The Insight approach suggests that the successful solution of a problem is dependent upon the arrangement of that problem in the perceiver's mind, while the Latent approach suggests we have a latent ability to learn which manifests itself when certain 'rewards' are presented.
5. Memory consists of three stages — sensory, short-term and long-term memory — each possessing its own distinctive attributes.

3.6 EXAM QUESTIONS

1. Compare and contrast Classical and Operant Conditioning.
2. Distinguish between the Cognitive and Connectionist approaches to learning. Give examples of each in your answer.
3. How can we improve our memory? Explain with reference to Atkinson and Shiffrin's model of memory.
4. What are the major stages of memory? Explain the length and capacity of each. Suggest some reasons that we forget.
5. Suggest some ways in which an understanding of Behaviourist learning principles could be of use to a marketing executive.

4

Motivation

4.1 INTRODUCTION

4.2 STATE AND TRAIT MOTIVATION

4.3 DRIVES
4.3.1 Unlearned and learned drives
4.3.2 Positive and negative drives

4.4 RESPONSES TO FRUSTRATION

4.5 TRADITIONAL MOTIVATIONAL THEORY
4.5.1 Taylor

4.6 CONTENT THEORIES OF MOTIVATION
4.6.1 Maslow's Hierarchy of Needs
4.6.2 McClelland's Need Theory
4.6.3 McGregor's Theory X and Theory Y
4.6.4 Herzberg's Two-Factor Theory

4.7 PROCESS THEORIES OF MOTIVATION
4.7.1 Vroom and Expectancy Theory
4.7.2 Adams and Equity Theory

4.8 MOTIVATION RESEARCH

4.9 SUMMARY

4.10 EXAM QUESTIONS

Learning Objectives

After studying this chapter you should be able to:

— *Understand the differing definitions of motivation, and distinguish between motives, drives and needs*
— *Describe and explain responses to frustration*
— *Explain the 'Content' theorists' approach to motivation*
— *Explain the 'Process' theorists' approach to motivation*
— *Describe motivational research methodologies.*

4.1 INTRODUCTION

Our understanding of motivation can lead to ambiguities. In one sense, motives are a particular class of reasons for doing something — as in a motive for murder. In another — broader — sense, motive refers to that which may cause an individual to behave in a consistent, sustained and organised fashion.

From a psychological perspective we are interested in the second, wider, understanding of the term. We use as a starting-point that individuals are active and their activity is instigated by the possession of both a discernible direction (goal-seeking) and a measure of intensity (pursuance of goals with persistence). Such goal-directed behaviour derives from an interaction between (a) internal states, and (b) external stimulation.

We begin with a look at the various terms involved in motivation, describing their interrelationship and examining what happens when motivation is hampered or obstructed, i.e. how we respond to frustration. We then move on to the various approaches to, and theories of, motivation. It is important to note that no theory is airtight, in that all theories have pluses and minuses. What we offer is a selection of the main theories of motivation divided into the 'Content' and 'Process' models. First we need to address the many concepts and definitions which arise from a study of motivation.

Motivation: basic and associated concepts

When the Olympics come around there is a spate of programmes on athletes' build-up to the games, showing how preparation and training takes its toll, financially and emotionally. We ask how they can push themselves to such extremes of mental and physical endurance. Is it to pursue excellence or to attain glory? We are questioning the role of motivation in their lives.

In studying motivation we attempt to answer such questions as:

(a) Why do some people seem more driven than others?

(b) Is this difference attributable to environment or upbringing? If the latter, can we influence the level of motivation in individuals?

(c) How much does the situation in which we find ourselves affect our level of motivation?

(d) Is it hard to motivate workers or potential consumers?

The study of motivation is important because of its psychological implications for human behaviour. A knowledge of motivational components can help us to gain a better insight into the 'why' of human behaviour.

Definition

A definition of motivation necessitates a definition of the terms 'drives' and 'needs'. It may help to illustrate by an example. On a warm summer's day we feel thirsty. Once we realise this is the case we decide to seek out a shop where we can buy thirst-quenching liquid. The thirst we feel is the **need**, our **motive** is to find a shop, and the strength of our need for liquid determines the strength of our **drive** to find a shop. If the need is strong enough, the drive will be correspondingly strong. Many definitions of motivation exist. Perhaps one of the most acceptable is that offered by Williams (1981): 'the interrelationship between needs, behaviour aimed at overcoming needs and the fulfilment of these needs'. In other words, motivation is a driving force that impels people into action.

4.2 STATE AND TRAIT MOTIVATION

The term 'state motivation' refers to the acquisition of a motive (of varying strength) from the particular state or situation in which one finds oneself. Returning to our Olympic athletes, they would experience 'state motivation' actually competing on the day, due to the atmosphere of the stadium and the presence of the fans. In fact the whole sense of occasion would contribute to their motivational state.

The difference between people in terms of strength of drives is called 'trait' motivation. The strength of an individual's motivation is not a function of the situation in which he finds himself but is dependent on the strength of his inherent motivational trait. In sport it is often not the person with the greater natural ability who wins, but the one who is more 'driven'. A sports writer summed this up when comparing two different types of footballer: 'Good players are *often* highly motivated, the best are *always* highly motivated.' McClelland (1961) has written extensively about this particular type of motivation, which we discuss later in the chapter. First, there are a number of important concepts to analyse before we examine a selection of motivational theorists offering varied and challenging motivational frameworks.

4.3 DRIVES

Drives are powerful motivating forces necessary for survival purposes. There is a distinction between learned and unlearned drives.

4.3.1 Unlearned and learned drives

Unlearned drives are innate, relate to our physiological survival, and include hunger, thirst and sleep. From the moment we are born we strive for fulfilment of these needs. While we can go for months without food, we cannot go without water or sleep for more than a few days. When the balance between these internal needs is upset, the body reacts by experiencing drives to satisfy these needs. The balance we return to is known as 'homoeostasis'. Because these drives are unlearned, primary and physiological in nature, regardless of individual or societal differences, all individuals experience similar sensations.

Learned drives, on the other hand, are social in nature and acquired by the socialisation process. Learned drives may take the form of needing to make friends, establishing sexual relationships and ultimately learning what role is expected of oneself in society, and expressing a drive to achieve it. They may be affected by such things as parental style, the ambient culture and personality factors. Whereas every human experiences the physiological needs described above, there may be enormous individual differences in learned drives. For example, individuals differ in their needs for social companionship and for approval.

4.3.2 Positive and negative drives

Positive drives motivate us to achieve a favourable outcome, such as an increase in our salary, or top marks in an exam. Advertisers aim to portray the acquisition of their products in terms of a positive drive, trying to convince consumers they will feel good once the product is bought.

Negative drives motivate us to avoid unpleasant outcomes. For example, a student facing a school test plays truant for the day. Advertisers try to persuade us to buy various types of toothbrushes or toothpastes on the grounds that we will thereby avoid dental problems.

The concept of drives offers the following combinations:

(a) **positive learned drives**   wanting to meet people, have a successful career

(b) **positive unlearned drives**   wanting to eat and drink when we are hungry

(c) **negative learned drives**   wanting to avoid a visit to the dentist or the doctor

(d) **negative unlearned drives**   wanting to avoid pain, e.g. when we put our hand too close to a fire we pull it away quickly and instinctively when we start to feel the pain.

4.4 RESPONSES TO FRUSTRATION

In examining motivation one must investigate not just how individuals perform in optimum conditions, but also how they react to obstacles and frustrations. The study of responses to frustration enhances the study of motivation and can show us the power of the frustrated drive. The level of frustration we feel is often related to the strength of the drive; for example, if we had worked ten hours a day over a year in order to do well in an exam and only passed, we would be very disappointed and frustrated.

The following are some ways in which Freud suggested we respond to frustration:

(a) **Compensation:** We often attempt to 'make up' to ourselves for a failure or disappointment. For example, if an individual is frustrated in an attempt to attain an executive position in the local tennis club, he may compensate for this by working harder in his career in order to derive a sense of achievement.

(b) **Regression:** When behaviour is thwarted we may find it difficult to cope with the consequences, and we regress or return to previously experienced secure states or modes of behaviour. Children often display regressive behaviour, such as thumb-sucking, when disciplined by parents.

(c) **Repression:** When denied the opportunity to attain a strongly desired goal, the individual may repress his desire to achieve. This is effectively a form of denial, which seeks to shut out from the individual's conscious mind the fact that the goal could not be attained.

(d) **Projection:** We often realise that some of our drives are socially unacceptable and may avoid this realisation by ascribing these views to others. Some people like soap operas but feel it is socially unacceptable to admit it so they project this 'liking' onto others.

(e) **Problem-solving behaviour:** When we experience frustration we may decide on alternative ways of achieving a goal. For example, roadworks can prevent us from travelling a particular route so we select an alternative rather than be annoyed with the situation.

(f) **Apathy:** We may simply give up and do nothing rather than choosing to react.

(g) **Aggression:** Aggression can take a number of forms:

(i) **constructive**, whereby we redouble our efforts to achieve a particular goal, as a rugby team may try doubly hard when being held up at the goal-line of their opponents

(ii) **destructive**, which aims to eliminate the persons or obstacles impeding the achievement of a goal. This is negative by its very nature. In the rugby example it might involve (1) the team using foul play to try to cross the line (direct destructive behaviour), or (2) after leaving the field, being rude to their trainer (indirect destructive behaviour). Indirect destructive behaviour is used by a worker who experiences difficulty in the workplace and takes out his frustrations on his spouse and family.

(h) **Rationalisation:** If we fail to obtain a job, we often rationalise this frustration in terms of interviewer bias.

Having dealt with a general overview of the term motivation, we now proceed to examine specific theories of motivation.

4.5 TRADITIONAL MOTIVATIONAL THEORY

4.5.1 Taylor

F.W. Taylor is considered the father of 'scientific management' principles and the most significant theorist under the banner of traditional management theories. His 'Principles of Scientific Management' were adopted within many organisations, setting the framework for what became known as job specialisation. Briefly, Taylor's distinct phases are:

(i) identification of task and employment of team

(ii) task analysis and job specialisation

(iii) task assignment and training

(iv) continued supervision, co-ordination and planning.

Taylor felt that only when a secure, tightly controlled framework was in place (providing employees with strict guidelines) could motivation be encouraged. He posited the notion that money was a prime motivator of work performance, with employees responding to the offer of more money by working proportionately harder (Taylor, 1947).

He tested his theories on a railway worker called Schmidt (Taylor, 1947), whose job it was to load iron onto trains. The average amount of iron loaded per day by each of the 75 workers at the depot was 12.5 tons. Taylor calculated that with the right incentive he could get Schmidt to load between 47 and 48 tons per day. He offered Schmidt a bonus depending on how much he loaded, and observed him over a period of three years. Taylor noted a significant improvement in performance, to 47 tons per day. Taylor's views are widespread, particularly amongst employers.

The obvious corollary is that given the right monetary incentive, employees will work harder — with little or no reference to such as (a) how they are made feel in their jobs, (b) working conditions, and (c) respect from management. A further implication is that employees can work harder, but will do so only for extra money. Many employers have taken this to mean that employees are lazy or that they are trying to get paid as much as they possibly can before being as productive as they can.

It should be remembered that:

(a) Taylor framed his theory of scientific management when labour was cheap, the workforce badly paid and operating in primitive working conditions. Against this background, it is easy to see how the workforce would be so motivated by money.

(b) Schmidt, being muscular, was exceptionally well suited to a labourer's job. Others may not be as well suited physically or mentally to their jobs, and so may not be able to improve their performance significantly.

4.6 CONTENT THEORIES OF MOTIVATION

Content or Need theories place emphasis on what actually motivates the worker or ordinary person. They identify what workers need, the strength of the needs and how workers will behave in order to satisfy these needs. We examine the following Content or Need theorists:

(i) Maslow

(ii) McClelland

(iii) Herzberg

(iv) McGregor.

The first of these is perhaps the best known, and his work is often remembered for the diagrams it spawned, namely Maslow's Hierarchy of Needs.

4.6.1 Maslow's Hierarchy of Needs

Abraham Maslow's work centred on the belief that our needs are hierarchical in nature, whereby certain basic needs such as hunger and thirst must be fulfilled before the individual can contemplate moving on to fulfil other, higher order needs, such as a need for self-esteem.

The famous hierarchy, represented in a pyramidic fashion below, contains an individual's progressive needs (which appear from the bottom up):

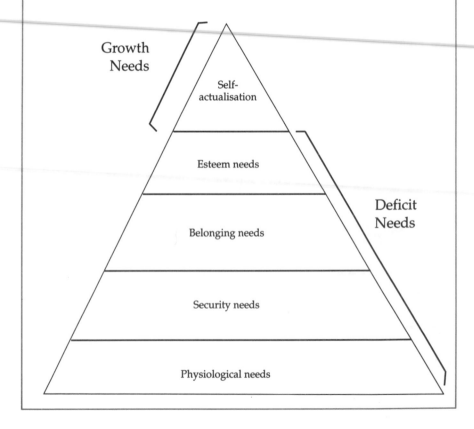

Deficit and growth needs

The bottom four on the hierarchy are termed the deficit needs and the top one the growth need, so called because without the former we experience social and physiological deficits without which we would not grow.

(a) **Physiological needs:** These are our basic needs, such as hunger, thirst and sleep. They are unlearned and must be satisfied before we can think about satisfying any other types of drive. African societies are often concerned predominantly with these needs because of famine in their lands. They have little time, therefore, to be concerned with higher order needs.

(b) **Security needs:** Most people crave a structure in their lives. They have learned security needs, such as order and stability, which find expression in law and order and a sense of personal security. Citizens in newly emerging countries are often concerned with the establishment of an ordered society.

(c) **Belonging needs:** These refer to learned social needs, finding expression in the need for love, affection and affiliation. Most Western societies provide an opportunity for their citizens to seek fulfilment of these belonging needs.

(d) **Esteem needs:** As learned social needs, esteem needs have to do with the need for appreciation from one's peers, symbolising the need for prestige and success. Usually this need finds expression in our working lives, where our salary can often engender respect and admiration from those around us.

(e) **Self-Actualisation:** Probably a minority of people realise their true potential; the rest do not self-actualise. Most people (a) are unable, (b) do not feel themselves able, or (c) are not in a position to take the road to self-discovery.

According to Maslow, we must fulfil one set of needs before we can, or would want to, embark on fulfilling the next set. For example, individuals trying to fulfil the needs on rung one of the hierarchy are not concerned with self-esteem needs, or self-actualising needs.

It is interesting to observe how organisational theorists have adapted Maslow's hierarchy in terms of employee fulfilment:

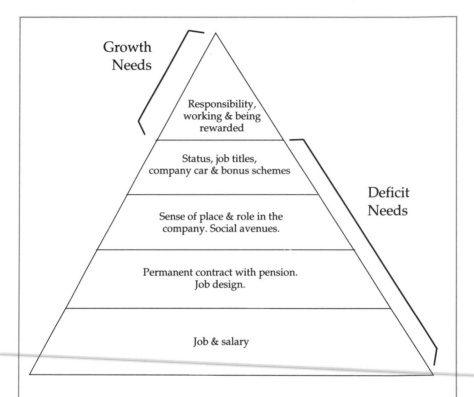

Maslow's hierarchy is also utilised from a marketing perspective, where marketing campaigns address each section of needs as being met by that product. For example, buying 'Beauty' soap will fulfil needs as follows:

(a) it will keep you clean (physiological needs)

(b) it has long-lasting effects (security needs)

(c) only those people who care about their skin buy this product (belonging needs)

(d) only the most discerning and youthful-looking people buy this product (self-esteem)

(e) if you buy this, who knows what it might lead to! (self-actualisation).

From both an organisational and marketing viewpoint, it is not strictly necessary to target each rung in the ladder (although a Maslow purist would disagree). Frequently a manager will try to fulfil only an employee's security needs while a marketing campaign might target the self-esteem needs.

4.6.2 McClelland's Need Theory

David C. McClelland agrees with the Need premise, but his theoretical framework encompasses only three needs:

(i) need for power

(ii) need for affiliation

(iii) need for achievement.

It is the third need to which we address ourselves as McClelland believed 'need for achievement' was the strongest and denoted an individual's level of motivation. To see exactly what he means by need for achievement we must examine where exactly he places its genesis.

There are, according to McClelland, two ways in which one's need for achievement develops:

(a) **Parental style:** McClelland states that our parents may imbue us with a positive attitude towards work and success. They may instil within us a desire to succeed, which transfers itself into a need, which in turn motivates us towards fulfilling and thus achieving behaviour.

(b) **Country of origin:** McClelland suggested that those who came from what were regarded as predominantly Protestant countries were more likely to display high need for achievement. He felt they had incorporated a Protestant 'work ethic' into their culture which affected every echelon of their society. McClelland (1961) attempted to support his assertions by pointing to the significantly larger amount of kilowatt hours consumed by factories in Protestant countries, as opposed to non-Protestant countries, thus supposedly displaying greater industriousness on the part of the former.

McClelland also stated here that those individuals displaying higher need for achievement were more likely to be engaged in enterprise, i.e. to be entrepreneurs. Further research has suggested that high need for achievement is not restricted to the entrepreneurial field, but also encompasses areas such as sport and politics. The common denominator between these areas, however, is that all the participants must have a lot of motivation in order to succeed.

From his studies McClelland suggested that those who have high need for achievement display the following traits:

(a) They prefer **working by themselves**, rather than having to submit themselves to the dictates of a superior. Personal responsibility is something desired by those displaying high need for achievement.

(b) They set themselves **moderate goals**, which are more realistic and have more chance of success.

(c) They are **realistic** and **seek out information** on their situation. This helps them to set the moderate goals above.

(d) They appreciate **regular feedback** on their activities.

The following diagram illustrates this relationship:

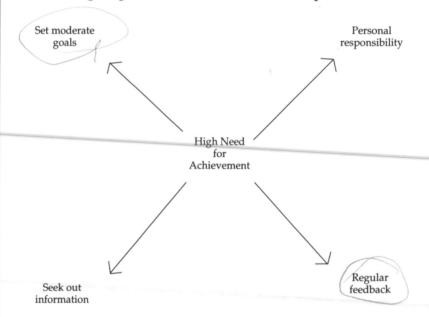

We turn next to theorists who have concentrated on the area of work and organisational motivation. These theorists are important because their ideas and beliefs are still operationalised in today's environment.

4.6.3 McGregor's Theory X and Theory Y

McGregor, a Need theorist similar to Maslow and McClelland, believed that motivation was obtained through fulfilment of employee needs. He disagreed with Taylorism, the traditional view of management, stating it had a very negative viewpoint of the worker in that it ignored workers' needs for fulfilment, and described them as lazy, indolent and solely motivated by either threats, punishment or monetary enticements. McGregor realised that this picture of the employee was one adopted by many organisations. He named it 'Theory X'.

Recognising that employees had needs such as self-fulfilment and responsibility, McGregor (1960) proposed a different view, labelled Theory Y, which conceptualises the worker as one who actively seeks self-fulfilment from his job and wants direction from others in how to achieve it. It further asserts that each worker is willing to take on more responsibility in an effort to solve problems within the organisation.

Many organisations employ Theory Y in their treatment of workers by investing in Human Resource Management (HRM), by giving employees facilities not dependent upon increased productivity and by employing less rigid management structures. Proponents of 'Theory Y' offer workers increased responsibility: for example, by appointing worker–directors and by soliciting the views of workers through 'suggestion boxes'.

4.6.4 Herzberg's Two-Factor Theory

Frederick Herzberg, a motivational theorist working in the late 1950s and early 1960s, recognised the value of 'Need' theories within organisational life. He developed the 'Two-Factor theory' of motivation, so called because he recognised two separate sets of factors affecting work motivations.

His research involved using the Critical Incident Technique, where 200 engineers and accountants were asked to relate work incidences in which they felt particularly good or bad about their jobs. Responses clearly defined two sets of factors: satisfiers (motivating factors) and dissatisfiers (hygiene factors).

Hygiene factors are not so much motivational factors as maintenance factors. In other words, if any of these are absent, dissatisfaction will ensue. If they are present, employees will experience neither dissatisfaction nor motivation, and be merely 'satisfied' with their job. These factors preventing dissatisfaction, called dissatisfiers, do not promote motivation. If workers are unhappy with such basic aspects of their jobs as salary, interpersonal relationships and security, it can produce dissatisfaction and lead to industrial disputes.

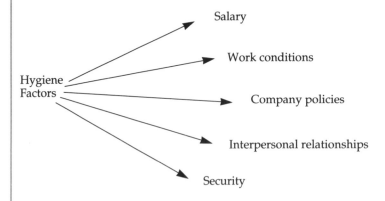

On the other hand, workers can be motivated to enhance their performance by what Herzberg (1959, 1974) termed 'motivating factors', such as responsibility, personal advancement and a sense of achievement. An employer does not have to supply these but if present they will lead to greater employee satisfaction and motivation, and therefore they are known as 'satisfiers'.

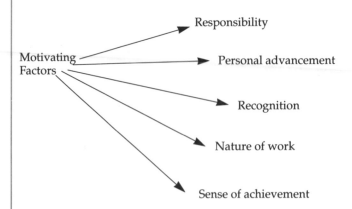

Note that hygiene factors tend to involve those factors related to the work environment while the motivating factors tend to involve job content. The interactiveness between the two can be represented thus:

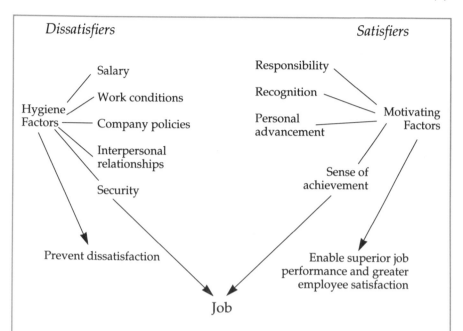

Herzberg's theory makes three assumptions:

(a) that employees are not motivated by monetary reward

(b) that employees require job content and motivators to experience satisfaction

(c) that the absence of hygiene factors leads to dissatisfaction only.

4.7 PROCESS THEORIES OF MOTIVATION

Where content theorists identified and focused on *what* motivated the worker, process theorists believe that motivation is actually a dynamic process of initiating and directing behaviours. In this section we deal with two process theorists:

(i) Vroom

(ii) Adams.

4.7.1 Vroom and Expectancy Theory

Vroom proposed a model of motivation based on three variables: valence, instrumentality and expectancy. The theory as a whole is based on the supposition that workers prefer a favourable to a less favourable outcome and will become motivated to ensure one. Favourability is the result of the interaction of valence, instrumentality and expectancy:

(a) **Valence:** If a person is attracted to a particular outcome, it possesses a positive valence, whereas if he is negative about the result it possesses a negative valence. If he is indifferent towards the outcome, a zero valence is recognised. The three states above might correspond to the offer of a salary increase, the request to do overtime, and the suggestion that the workers' offices be painted in a pastel colour.

(b) **Instrumentality:** In this, Vroom distinguished between first-level outcomes (which are performance-related) and second-level outcomes (which are need-related). Vroom suggested that the extent to which workers attempt first-level outcomes is a result of how important the second-level outcome is to them. The prospect of a pay increase (second-level outcome) may motivate them highly in their work (first-level outcome). It is the strength of the linkage between the first- and second-level outcomes which determines their effectiveness. In this respect, they can be rated from +1 (strong linkage) to –1 (weak linkage).

(c) **Expectancy:** This is the extent to which the person being motivated believes there is a chance or probability of a particular outcome. This could be the probability that the managing director will provide a place on the board. If the worker does not believe this will happen his motivation is affected accordingly. Expectancy can range from '0' (which sees no chance of the event happening) to '1' (indicating certainty that a particular outcome will be reached).

Vroom suggested that the above can be framed in this equation, where 'M' stands for motivation, which is a function of the valences ('V') times the strength of the expectancies ('E'):

$$M = \sum (E \times V).$$

An example of Vroom's Theory can be seen in the following activity, from Buchanan and Huczynski (1991):

First: List the outcomes that you expect will result from your working hard for the present course, such as:

(a) High exam marks

(b) Bare pass

(c) Sleepless nights

(d) No social life.

Second: Rate the value you place on each of these outcomes, giving those you like +1, those you dislike –1, and those about which you are neutral 0. These are your 'V' values.

Third: Estimate the probability of attaining each of these outcomes, giving those that are certain the value 1, those that are most unlikely the value 0, and those for which there is an even chance the value 0.5. Estimate other probabilities as you perceive them at other values between 0 and 1. These are your 'E' values.

Fourth: Now put your E and V values into the expectancy equation

$$M = \sum (E \times V)$$

and add up the result.

Fifth: Compare your M score with the scores of your colleagues. We predict that:

* those with higher scores are the course 'swots'

* those with the higher scores will get higher exam marks.

Finally, while well framed, Vroom's Theory has not received strong empirical support (Galbraith and Cummings, 1967), though the same research showed (somewhat like Mayo's findings in the Hawthorne Studies; see 7.6.4) that the valence of workers' duties increased when they perceived that the instrumentality of attention (from their supervisors) increased. In other words, they worked harder if they felt they would receive more attention from their supervisors.

4.7.2 Adams and Equity Theory

Adams suggested that worker satisfaction is a result of equity being achieved between their inputs (effort, training, ability) and their outputs (salary, status, and job benefits), as illustrated by the diagram below. Perceived inequity may be a result of a perceived disparity in the ratio of inputs to outputs — not just that the inputs outweigh the outputs. To arrive at this conclusion, Adams suggests that workers actively compare their lot with that of others in a similar position. The inequity is a function not just of their own inputs and outputs, but also of how they perceive the equity or inequity of the other situation.

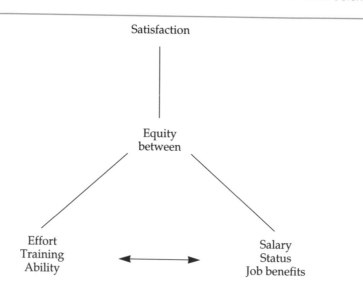

There are a number of ways that employees can react to perceived inequity. If they feel they are being under-rewarded they may work less hard, seek greater reward or produce goods of a lower quality. On the other hand, if they feel they are being over-rewarded they may work harder, take a deduction in their wages or improve the quality of the goods produced. This would indicate that increased worker recognition leads to greater job satisfaction and greater productivity. The organisational culture of many Irish firms during the 1970s was not open to input from workers and neither management nor workers seemed willing to analyse their respective inputs and outputs. Further, many workers' demands centred on the perceived inequity of their pay, as compared with other workers in the same industry. This led to a large amount of industrial disputes.

4.8 MOTIVATION RESEARCH

Even though the majority of motivation research carried out nowadays is in the area of marketing (why consumers buy particular products), its genesis was in the field of psychology. This is an important point as some researchers feel that its involvement in marketing has produced a one-dimensional theory of people's motivations, i.e. as consumers. We look here at some of the ways in which we may examine people's motivations. These tests are in the main derived from clinical psychology and are usually of a projective nature. This means that an individual is not called on to state explicitly what his feelings are on a particular issue, but rather reveals them by how he responds to certain test cues with which he is presented:

(a) **Thematic Apperception Test (TAT):** The person is shown a drawing or photograph and asked to make up a story about it. For example, in the TAT — which can measure need for achievement — people are presented with a picture of an executive in an office looking at a picture of his spouse and children. High need for achievement responses to this stimulus would emphasise a strongly driven executive supported and encouraged by his family. Low need for achievement responses would include emphasis on the executive's loneliness in the work environment, away from a family whom he misses.

(b) **Rorschach Test:** In what is usually known as the 'ink-blot' test, the subject is presented with a number of brightly coloured ink-blot-type figures and asked to reply spontaneously as to what he thinks the ink blots look like. The test examines imagination, originality and the variety of thoughts. It can often be useful in examining deep-seated feelings and emotions. A variation is used in marketing research when a consumer is asked for spontaneous reactions to new designs for packaging.

(c) **Word Association Test:** Developed by the psychiatrist Carl Gustav Jung, this test presents the subject with single words asking him to respond with the first word that enters his head. It is designed to examine the mental associations an individual possesses, in a quick, easily accessible manner. This can also be used in a marketing sphere to test what consumers think about a new product.

(d) **Research questionnaire:** This is one of the primary instruments used by all researchers to test attitudes. It may be administered in person, on the street or in the home, or sent through the post. It can be a very powerful tool in quantifying the strength and magnitude of individuals' feelings towards products, social issues or services.

An understanding of motivation is important in comprehending actions in all spheres of life. Study of the topic provides insights into how exactly people are motivated or how it is possible to accommodate people's needs and expectations. We have also seen here that workers are not motivated to work harder purely by the offer of more money, but rather by complex factors such as the respect they receive from their workmates and superiors.

4.9 SUMMARY

1. Motivation is the interrelationship between needs, behaviour aimed at overcoming needs and the fulfilment of these needs, and is a driving force that impels people into action.
2. Drives are powerful motivating forces which impel us towards realising needs. The perceived importance and strength of needs vary from person to person.
3. Responses to frustration can often be in the form of defence mechanisms, such as problem-solving, aggression and rationalisation.
4. Study of motivation is divided between Need or Content theorists and Process theorists. The former include Maslow, McClelland, Herzberg and McGregor. The latter include Vroom and Adams.
5. Common research methods into motivation include the TAT, the Rorschach Test, Jung's Word Association Test and the research questionnaire.

4.10 EXAM QUESTIONS

1. In relation to Maslow's theory of motivation, present a definition of motivation and show how it might usefully be applied to a work, marketing or organisational situation.
2. Compare and contrast the main organisational theories of motivation.
3. Explain the principal aspects of McClelland's theory of motivation. In your opinion does it present a credible theory of what motivates human beings?
4. Describe the main ways in which we react to being frustrated. In your answer you should provide examples of each of the coping mechanisms you present.
5. Examine the chief similarities and differences between Need and Process theories of motivation.

Attitudes

5.1　INTRODUCTION

5.2　ATTITUDES: POSSIBLE DEFINITIONS
　　5.2.1 Characteristics of attitudes

5.3　FUNCTIONS OF ATTITUDES

5.4　SOURCES OF ATTITUDES

5.5　TRICOMPONENT ATTITUDE MODEL

5.6　ATTITUDES AND BEHAVIOUR

5.7　ATTITUDE MEASUREMENT
　　5.7.1 Introduction
　　5.7.2 Semantic differential scale
　　5.7.3 Thurstone scale
　　5.7.4 Likert scale
　　5.7.5 Guttman's Scalogram Analysis

5.8　CONSISTENCY MODELS OF ATTITUDES
　　5.8.1 Balance theory
　　5.8.2 Cognitive Dissonance theory
　　5.8.3 Congruity theory

5.9　FISHBEIN'S THEORY OF REASONED ACTION
　　5.9.1 Fishbein's First Model (1967)
　　5.9.2 Fishbein's Extended Model (1975)

5.10 ATTITUDE CHANGE

5.11 SUMMARY

5.12 EXAM QUESTIONS

Learning Objectives

After studying this chapter you should be able to:

— *Understand the major definitions of attitudes*
— *Describe the characteristics, components, functions and sources of attitudes*
— *Understand attitudinal measurement scales*
— *Discuss consistency models of attitudes*
— *Explain and evaluate the variables concerned with attitude change.*

5.1 INTRODUCTION

The attitudes we hold affect most aspects of our lives — our behaviours, opinions, friendships, motives and learnings. Attitudes are basically how we feel about something. A knowledge of attitudes is important if we wish to understand human behaviour. If we gain insight into how and why attitudes are formed we may understand others' views and actions. Attitudes often indicate how we feel about something: for example, attitudes towards authority, towards social issues, towards responsibility. The difficulty with studying attitudes (as with so many psychological topics) is that they are a hypothetical construct and therefore unseen, so we have to infer the presence of an attitude from a person's behaviour.

Within organisational spheres, attitudes frequently determine the general approach of an employee to work — in terms of conscientiousness, motivation or responsibility. Within marketing spheres, whenever consumers are asked to express their feelings about a product or service, they are being asked to express their attitudes.

In this chapter we hope to examine a number of attitudinal aspects — what they consist of, how they are acquired, what purposes they serve. We also introduce a number of attitudinal models and methodologies developed by behavioural scientists in an attempt to put some sort of measurement into the subject.

5.2 ATTITUDES: POSSIBLE DEFINITIONS

Researchers have devoted much effort to defining attitudes, in order to differentiate them from views, beliefs and other cognitive processes. The following are a sample of the definitions.

Kretch and Crutchfield (1948) defined an attitude as 'an enduring organisation of motivational, emotional, perceptual and cognitive processes with respect to some aspect of the individual's world'. They described an attitude as a wide umbrella of interactions towards the world, embracing feelings such as sadness, motivation and happiness.

Gordon Allport (1954) defined an attitude as 'a mental and neural state of readiness, organised through experience, exerting a directive or dynamic influence upon the individual's response to all situations and situations with which it is related'. Allport describes an attitude as a dynamic force, involving interactions with the outside world. This approach differs slightly from Kretch and Crutchfield's in that Allport views us as being ready at all times to express our attitudes by what we do and say.

Kretch, Crutchfield and Ballachey (1962) later defined an attitude as 'an enduring system of positive or negative evaluations, emotional feeling and pro or con action states towards a social object'. This seeks to narrow the range of attitudes to within our social sphere.

An attitude is a somewhat complex phenomenon, involving factors such as **beliefs**, where we accept that something is true, e.g. statements about relationships ('I have a good employer'), and **values**, which are special types of beliefs often expressed as: abstract ideals ('I think marriage is a sacred institution'); ideal modes of conduct (e.g. honesty and loyalty); and ideal goals (e.g. happiness, equality and security).

Our attitude towards divorce, for example, may be an interaction of our belief system (belief in the strength of the family unit) and value system (considering fidelity and loyalty significant tenets in all human relationships). Naturally, our past experiences, environment and important 'others' in our lives affect how we feel towards any particular object/situation. Attitudes, therefore, embrace many of the factors in the following diagram:

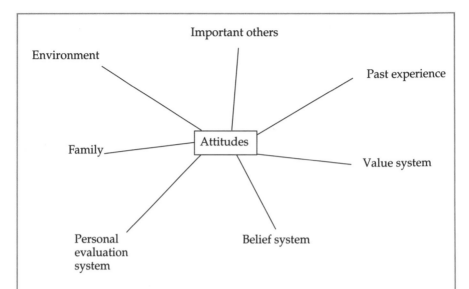

Put simply, an attitude is an inclination to perceive, interpret and evaluate people, events and issues in a certain manner.

5.2.1 Characteristics of attitudes

Attitudes have several important characteristics:

(a) **They are learned:** We are not born with attitudes, we learn them primarily from the family (our first socialising group) and from society at large.

(b) **They are persistent:** Unlike a mood, attitudes will persist over time. We see evidence of this in Iran's attitude towards Salman Rushdie, where the intensity of their negative attitude has not wavered over the years.

(c) **They are predictive of behaviour:** Because an attitude expresses how someone feels, it can be used as a measure of behavioural predictability. Opinions differ here, some psychologists believing that attitudes suggest only a general pattern of behaviour rather than specific, predictable actions.

(d) **They can exist at low levels of consciousness:** Frequently an individual is unaware of how strongly he feels towards a situation until a discussion is entered into, or he is required to vote on or contribute to a topic.

(e) **They retain the uniqueness of human experience:** The individuality of the person plays a big part in the expression of attitudes. Many people may share a similar attitude, but differ in expression and/or behaviour simply because of the uniqueness of their experience.

5.3 FUNCTIONS OF ATTITUDES

Daniel Katz (1960) introduced the notion of psychologically dynamic functions of attitudes. He suggested that these functions provide a motivational basis for behaviours in terms of predisposing a person either positively or negatively towards situations. That is, we hold particular attitudes for a particular psychological reason.

(a) **Adjustment function** directs people towards satisfying, favourable and positive rewards and away from dissatisfying and unfavourable punishments. It directs an individual to express an attitude which will be favourably received by society (thus gaining approval, i.e. a reward) and enables him to adjust or move away from the expression of an attitude that might be greeted with disapproval (punishment). A politician might be careful not to espouse racially discriminatory attitudes in case he loses support.

(b) **Ego-defensive function** protects one's self-image from threatening information. Rather than disclose our perceived, or real, failings to ourselves, we adopt an ego-defensive attitude. For example, a person who makes a poor career judgment may adopt an aggressive attitude and defend his 'mistake' by saying he was misled by colleagues.

(c) **Value-expressive function** permits us to express strongly held beliefs and values, which in turn discloses our inner selves to other people. These values/beliefs say a lot about us, and what type of people we are. People will often adopt certain attitudes in order to communicate their self-image. For example, people serving voluntarily in war-torn areas such as Bosnia are expressing their value systems. It is not sufficient for them to sympathise or donate financially, they wish to exercise their caring attitude in a more tangible manner.

(d) **Knowledge function** is a product of people's need for stability, coherence and consistency in their lives. For example, in order to feel secure we need a job and a place to live. Our knowledge function guides our feelings and behaviours in such a way as to ensure, to the best of our ability, that neither of these will in any way threaten the likelihood of security, by displaying either inappropriate behaviour (being late) or inappropriate feelings (sarcasm to the boss).

5.4 SOURCES OF ATTITUDES

As we know, attitudes are not innate; we learn or acquire them in many ways, from many sources:

(a) **Family:** This is a major influence in an individual's life. Here attitudes are absorbed, almost unconsciously, and are rarely questioned. This is our first experience of interaction with other people, so we learn from it.

(b) **Influential others:** These include reference groups, peers, friends, whose opinions we seek out and which are important to us. The influence of these others is quite profound, because we respect their judgments and tend to adopt similar views through a need to identify with them.

(c) **Interaction and direct experience:** We come into contact with situations constantly, causing us at times to re-evaluate our thoughts or views. For example, our attitude towards people with a mental handicap may have originally been fairly negative (e.g. frightened of them), yet through a friendship scheme, whereby we can meet and interact with such people, our attitude changes to a more positive frame of mind.

(d) **Mass media:** In today's world the media have a profound influence on society. We are directed, cajoled and intimidated into forming attitudes. For instance, many young girls have adopted an attitude towards their bodies which the media have supplied: to be thin is to be attractive. Obviously there are deeper psychological reasons involved, but the media must claim responsibility for reinforcing the attitude towards a 'perfect' shape.

There are other sources contributing towards attitude function. The following diagram illustrates a range of these sources.

Remember that there is a dynamic interaction between internal and external forces.

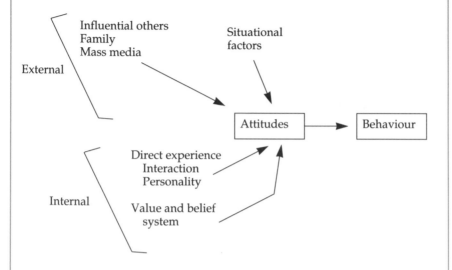

5.5 TRICOMPONENT ATTITUDE MODEL

Attitudes are often portrayed as consisting of three major components: cognitive component, affective component and conative component.

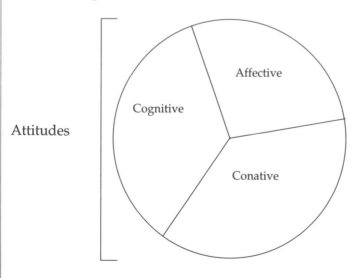

(a) **Cognitive component** consists of knowledge and perceptions an individual possesses in relation to the attitudinal object. This component concerns the belief/disbelief element of an attitude. We use our thought processes to decide whether a manufacturer's claim that its lotion produces a miracle cure for baldness is really credible.

(b) **Affective component** consists of a person's overall evaluation of the situation. This component refers to the emotions and feelings element of an attitude. For example, the idea of using the hair lotion highlights our feelings about hair loss and perhaps poor self-image.

(c) **Conative component** refers to the readiness to respond or the likelihood of our response to the attitudinal object. Will we undertake a specific action, i.e. go and buy the product?

5.6 ATTITUDES AND BEHAVIOUR

We have seen the tricomponent model of an attitude encompassing the concept of an action component, or a readiness to respond component. Next we must ask how attitudes are linked to behaviour? Some behavioural scientists believe that the link between action and attitudes is at best tenuous — an expression of an attitude is not necessarily consistent with behaviour. Others believe that there is a very definite connection and that from attitudes we can not only infer but also predict behaviours. At most, the link between attitudes and behaviour is interactive, with a number of variables influencing this relationship:

(a) **Intensity:** The stronger and more intense the attitude the less it will be compromised, and the more predictive it is of behaviour. For example, a person with a strong Catholic attitude to divorce will probably vote against its introduction into Ireland.

(b) **Existence of other attitudes:** The existence of a strong attitude may frequently inhibit the behavioural expression of a weaker attitude. For example, an individual may hold that equality is important regardless of class yet have a far stronger attitude towards law and order. This might mean that he would support tougher policing in high crime areas, even though this may interfere with certain civil rights.

(c) **Ability to respond:** Learning to respond to a particular attitude is often conditioning. Family, peers and life experience tend to reinforce our long-held attitudes. Therefore our ability to respond in any novel way is doubtful.

(d) **Situational factors:**

(i) **physical environment:** The environment can sometimes inhibit behavioural expression of an attitude, e.g. it would be rather foolhardy to denounce Hell's Angels as the source of evil in the world if one were surrounded by them.

(ii) **social environment:** Sensibilities of others frequently prevent individuals from expressing their true feelings, e.g. one's attitude to animal testing for medical purposes might be somewhat subdued by the presence of 'animal liberators'.

5.7 ATTITUDE MEASUREMENT

5.7.1 Introduction

In order to understand more fully the concept of attitudes it is necessary to examine the various attitude measurement approaches or scales. All approaches emphasise:

(a) the **direction of the attitude**, i.e. whether it is positive or negative or even indifferent

(b) the **degree** or extent to which the attitude is in that direction

(c) the **intensity of feeling** that goes with the attitude.

Scales differ in a number of ways:

(a) **Construction:** The manner in which attitudinal measures differ may be due to factors such as cost, accessibility to the target population and the nature of the attitudes being examined.

(b) **Response:** Tests differ in how people reply. In some cases they are asked to comply in varying degrees (e.g. strongly disagree) while in others they are asked dichotomous questions, prompting yes/no answers.

(c) **Dimensions:** With some attitudinal tests it is less the person's response on each item than the total score which matters. Respondents are differentiated by this score rather than by the pattern of their responses.

(d) **Scale differentiates:** People who are at different points along the scale are placed in various categories. The nature of these categories depends on the type of scale being used.

The two remaining differences between scales require a more thorough examination.

Firstly, scales are either **manifest** or **latent**. Manifest scales are those which are explicit in the attitude they are testing, with the respondent aware of what is under test. Latent scales refer to those scales where the subject does not know what attitudes are being examined. For example, the Californian F-scale examines respondents' underlying views towards fascism. This F-scale, rather than explicitly asking the respondents whether they approve of fascism, asks to what extent they agree with particular statements which are not overtly related to fascism but which test samples have shown to be connected. It discloses whether or not a high probability of displaying fascist tendencies is present.

There is also a distinction between **differential** and **summational** scales. In the former, subjects' responses are divided into whether they 'agree', 'disagree' or 'don't know'. Summational scales, on the other hand, add the scores for each of the responses and come up with a summated, or cumulative, score. Respondents are then compared with reference to the different scores they achieved.

The following five scales are a mixture of the differential and summational.

5.7.2 Semantic differential scale

Osgood's (1957) semantic differential scale uses bipolar adjectives to test attitudes. These adjectives are usually grouped by type, i.e. evaluation (good/bad, cold/warm, bright/dull), potency (strong/weak, hard/soft) and activity (active/passive, fast/slow). In all, these particular types of adjectives account for 50 per cent of the concept meaning. In theory any adjectives can be used, as long as they are bipolar in nature.

It is a typical seven-point scale, though three or five points may also be used. Some researchers suggest it is better to use a larger set of points because it allows the subtlety of the attitude to be brought out. For example, if testing people's attitudes towards hare-coursing, the use of a five- or seven-point scale allows a broader range or scope of answer, e.g. 'quite cruel', rather than 'very cruel'. Below is an example of a semantic differential questionnaire on people's attitudes towards television.

Television Questionnaire

The following are some adjectives which could be used to describe television. Please put a tick beside those adjectives you feel best describe television. Please tick beside all the adjectives.

	+2	+1	0	−1	−2	
Good	☐	☐	☐	☐	☐	Bad
Peaceful	☐	☐	☐	☐	☐	Violent
Original	☐	☐	☐	☐	☐	Unoriginal
Interesting	☐	☐	☐	☐	☐	Boring
Cheap	☐	☐	☐	☐	☐	Expensive
Stimulating	☐	☐	☐	☐	☐	Stultifying
Observant	☐	☐	☐	☐	☐	Clichéd
Exciting	☐	☐	☐	☐	☐	Mundane
Liberal	☐	☐	☐	☐	☐	Conservative
Concise	☐	☐	☐	☐	☐	Long-winded

Advantages and disadvantages

Some of the potential difficulties with this scale are the same as those examined in detail later with Likert's scale. Two people may understand different things when given the same adjective; for example, given the adjective 'violent', some parents may take it to mean abusive language, while others may interpret it as actual physical violence. Also, some people may not understand the adjectives being given but be too polite or too embarrassed to say so.

On the positive side, this is an extremely widely used test, it is easily constructed, easily understood and by virtue of being a differential scale it teases out the subtleties of a person's attitude by examining the pattern of his responses.

5.7.3 Thurstone scale

The Thurstone scale, developed by Thurstone and Chave in 1929, presents the respondent with a limited number of statements (perhaps between ten and twenty), each possessing a numerical value. The subject then indicates whether he agrees with any of the statements. The total of agreed statements is summed and the researcher has an idea of how the person views the attitudinal object.

The following is an example of the Thurstone scale, on attitudes towards religion.

Scale Value	Statement
0.5	I feel the Church is the greatest agency for the uplift of the world.
2.4	I feel the Church is trying to adjust itself to the scientific world and deserves support.
5.2	I am neither for nor against the Church but I do not believe that church-going will do anyone any harm.
8.0	I think the Church is petty, easily disturbed by matters of little importance.
11.0	I have nothing but contempt for the Church.

Advantages and disadvantages

The main disadvantage of this scale is that the initial collation of statements is expensive and its design is time-consuming and cumbersome, and so it tends not to be used much. However, it is accurate, and was conceived in the fledgling days of psychological research into attitudes.

5.7.4 Likert scale

Developed in 1932, the Likert scale is perhaps the most widely used attitudinal sampling method in either market or social science research. It presents prospective respondents with statements to which they have to signify the extent of their agreement, from 'strongly agree' through 'undecided' to 'strongly disagree'. There are a number of important points to remember when using this scale:

(a) **Language** of the statement should be simple, clear and direct. The respondent should be left in no doubt as to how to answer the statement.

(b) **Simple sentences** should be used instead of compound or complex ones.

(c) **Avoid ambiguous statements** as they may lead to confusion.

(d) **One complete thought** should be contained in each statement. Otherwise, respondents are being asked to respond to more than one question in any one statement.

(e) **Avoid statements which may be interpreted as factual**, making some respondents feel they cannot agree or disagree, e.g. 'The economy is improving.'

(f) **Avoid statements which would be endorsed by everyone**. This particularly applies to statements which wish for goodwill, or aspire to socially acceptable goals, e.g. 'World hunger should be reduced' or 'I am in favour of world peace.'

A Likert scale might look as follows, if one were testing consumers' attitudes towards a new product 'Softclean':

'Softclean' Product Questionnaire

1. Softclean cleans clothes without losing softness
Strongly agree ☐ Agree ☐ Undecided ☐ Disagree ☐ Strongly disagree ☐

2. There's no washing powder as effective as Softclean on the market
Strongly agree ☐ Agree ☐ Undecided ☐ Disagree ☐ Strongly disagree ☐

3. Softclean is the cheapest washing powder on the market
Strongly agree ☐ Agree ☐ Undecided ☐ Disagree ☐ Strongly disagree ☐

4. There are no ways in which Softclean could be improved
Strongly agree ☐ Agree ☐ Undecided ☐ Disagree ☐ Strongly disagree ☐

5. Softclean staff never deal with my customer queries
Strongly agree ☐ Agree ☐ Undecided ☐ Disagree ☐ Strongly disagree ☐

Advantages and disadvantages

Its disadvantages lie mainly in the danger that statements chosen for use may be flawed and unrepresentative. Further, it places a great responsibility on the researcher to devise and test out appropriate statements. However, the Likert scale is the most commonly used attitudinal scale in market research, and in psychology, because of its ease of construction, its relatively low cost in testing, and its straightforward method of data analysis.

5.7.5 Guttman's Scalogram Analysis

Guttman developed his Scalogram Analysis in 1950, basing it essentially on Bogardus's (1925) social distance scale, which placed great emphasis on the observation of social attitudes. This scale has been used both in social science and market research. Its idiosyncrasy lies less in what it tests than in the way it does so, with its distinctive ordering of statements — the relevance of which we examine later.

It is a cumulative, or summational, scale to which subjects are asked to respond in a dichotomous manner, i.e. yes or no. It remains a useful tool in examining groupings of social attitudes around a particular attitudinal object.

A typical social distance scale consists of the following types of questions, in the following type of order:

> **I would happily marry someone from a different culture and race to my own.**
> **I would have a coloured person as my best friend.**
> **I would live beside a coloured person.**
> **I would live in the same neighbourhood as a coloured person.**
> **I would work with a coloured person.**
> **I would eat in the same restaurant as a coloured person.**
> **I would stand beside a coloured person at a bus-stop.**
> **I would talk to a coloured person.**

This might in turn lead the market researcher to design the following questionnaire to test consumers' views of the clothes-washing market. The questionnaire presumes that from the point where the consumer responds negatively to an item, he will do so to every subsequent item:

Market Research Survey

We are interested in your views on products in the washing powder market. The question we would like you to consider is which of the following items you regard as essential in the care and cleaning of your clothes. Please answer 'Yes' or 'No' beside each item:

	Yes	No
Washing Machine	☐	☐
Tumble Drier	☐	☐
Washing Powder	☐	☐
Drier Towel	☐	☐
Fabric Conditioner	☐	☐

Advantages and disadvantages

It is all-important in this scale to achieve the correct administration order. Failure to do so may lead to inaccuracies in the measurement. To convert various attitudes into potential dichotomous responses can be a complicated and arduous process as some may not respond easily to this dichotomising. As a technique it is laborious, but good for examining small attitude shifts.

5.8 CONSISTENCY MODELS OF ATTITUDES

We examine here some of the more popular models of attitudes, umbrellaed under the heading 'consistency models'. Each of these models expresses a similar premise, i.e. that the individual seeks to achieve harmony or consistency in his attitudes and behaviour. If tension, upset or inconsistency is perceived, the individual strives to reduce this state of unease in order to return to a consistent state. The three models we discuss are: Balance theory, Cognitive Dissonance theory and Congruity theory.

5.8.1 Balance theory

This theory, posited by Heider (1946 and 1958), is concerned mainly with triadic relationships — i.e. one person receiving information from another about a particular object. Balance theory states that attitudes towards a person or persons will have positive or negative values, and that there is a tendency for values to change if the system becomes imbalanced, as this causes tension. Rather than suffer tension or inconsistency, the individual will seek consistency by changing an attitude.

For example, if we (A) hold the view that racism (B) is wrong, and we meet someone (C) whom we like but who believes in racial discrimination, we can either view the person we've met negatively, or change our views on racism. In this case the relationship would be imbalanced. Heider represented this type of relationship in a triangular form with a '+' standing for a positive view of some person or thing and a '–' standing for the opposite.

Balanced and imbalanced relationships can be represented in the following examples:

(a) *Balanced relationship*
Let us presume that we (A) held a positive view towards someone (B) and that they in turn held a positive attitude towards a particular object (C), and so did we. The relationship would look as follows:

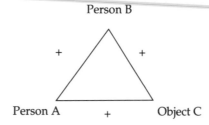

(b) *Imbalanced relationship*
If we suppose that we (A) view a person (B) negatively, that we view a particular object (C) negatively and that they also view the same object negatively, then the system is imbalanced. It would appear as follows:

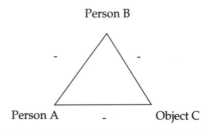

(c) *Imbalanced relationship*
Finally, if we (A) viewed a certain person (B) negatively, and we viewed a particular object positively — as they did — the relationship would look as follows:

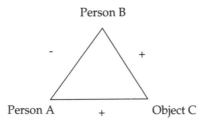

In the last two cases there is a pressure on the individual to change his view on aspects of the triangular relationship in order to ease the tension and achieve balance.

5.8.2 Cognitive Dissonance theory

Developed by Leon Festinger (1957), the theory of Cognitive Dissonance describes the cognitive upset or 'mental clashing' that occurs when a person recognises that two thoughts or actions (both held to be true by him) are inconsistent: in other words, they contradict each other. Similar to Heider in his Balance theory, Festinger believes that such a conflict results in tension, which in turn motivates the individual to action in an effort to restore harmony or consistency. Dissonance may be experienced by an individual when he realises there is inconsistency between an attitude and behaviour. For example, he may believe that smoking is one of the main contributors to lung cancer yet continue to smoke. It is important to note that dissonance occurs only if the person *himself* realises the inconsistency in his belief and behaviour. Many of us are able unconsciously to hold a contradictory element in our lives.

Dissonance theory has implications in consumer behaviour. For example, the dissonance a consumer feels is affected by some of the following factors:

(a) The more important the decision the greater the degree of potential dissonance. These decisions are known by marketers as 'High-Involvement Decisions' and are usually ones entailing a substantial emotional or financial input.

(b) The more alternatives exist, the greater the potential dissonance.

(c) If there is very little difference between the alternatives there is much greater chance of dissonance.

(d) The greater the amount of negative aspects of the goods chosen, the greater the potential dissonance.

The opposite of dissonance is consonance, which Festinger believes we try to achieve where possible. Consumers can achieve this in a number of ways:

(a) The decision can be changed, with the consumer returning the goods or buying the rejected alternative.

(b) The consumer can emphasise the positive aspects and minimise the negative aspects of the goods he has bought.

(c) The consumer can emphasise more the negative aspects of the rejected alternative and reject or ignore its positive aspects.

(d) Attitudes or beliefs can be changed in order to be consistent with behaviour.

5.8.3 Congruity theory

Developed by Osgood et al. (1957), this theory defines consistency as congruity, stipulating that if an individual suffered tension as a result of holding conflicting attitudes or beliefs, something would change in order to re-create a consistency or congruity. Congruity and incongruity are perhaps better explained through the use of the following diagrams:

(a) *Congruity*
If a football player whom we admire greatly (say giving a +3 on the following scale) endorses and praises a particular pair of boots which we have ourselves, and which we also like (+3 on the scale), there is no discrepancy — both attitudes are at the same point on the scale.

−3	−2	−1	0	+1	+2	+3
						x
						(a) Own boots
						(b) Footballer's endorsement

(b) *Incongruity*

If a celebrity whom we like (+2) endorses a product we didn't particularly like (–2), the amount of incongruity is equal on each side and so will be reduced by equal amounts on each side to '0'.

–3	–2	–1	0	+1	+2	+3
		0 >>>>>>>>>>>> 0 <<<<<<<<<<<< 0				
	Object				Person	

(c) *Incongruity*

If someone whom we love and trust very much, say a spouse or best friend (+3 on the scale), expresses a negative opinion about a subject on which we hold an opinion (–1), our attitude will change in favour of the more strongly held attitude. In this case our attitude will change in the direction of the attitude we hold regarding our spouse or best friend. So the less strongly held attitude will probably change from –1 to +2, and our opinion of our spouse or best friend will change from +3 to +2, as we know that he is not an acknowledged expert on the subject.

–3	–2	–1	0	+1	+2	+3
		0 >>>>>>>>>>>>>>>>>>>>0 <<<< 0				
		Object				Person

There may be little or no change in some cases. For example:

(a) if the person receiving the information does not believe it, his attitude will not change

(b) if he only marginally disbelieves what he is presented with, his attitude change will not be great.

5.9 FISHBEIN'S THEORY OF REASONED ACTION

A theorist who offers a multiattribute model of attitudes, of particular use within a marketing sphere, is Fishbein. His treatment of consumer behaviour is far more sophisticated than any of our previous consistency models. Fishbein recognised the interactiveness between beliefs and information in relation to the attitudinal object, and suggested two major models to explain the complexity of consumers' attitudes to particular products.

5.9.1 Fishbein's First Model (1967)

Fishbein's first attitudinal model of reasoned action suggests that one's attitude towards an object is a function of the sum of the various composites of that attitude, weighted by the evaluation one gives to each of the composites. Fishbein also believed that people form attitudes towards objects on the basis of their **beliefs** (perceptions and knowledge) about these objects. Positive or negative feelings are also formed on the basis of these beliefs. Therefore, Fishbein's model is constructed so that in a person's overall attitude some object is derived from his beliefs and feelings about various attributes of the object. This is represented by the following formula, which incorporates the cognitive (belief) and affective (evaluation) components of attitudes:

$$A_o = \sum_{i=1}^{n} b_i a_i$$

where:

Ao = the attitude towards the object o

bi = the strength of belief i about o

ai = the evaluation aspects of b

n = the number of beliefs.

Take, for example, an attempt to evaluate the attitude of customers to the Minitel service provided by An Bord Telecom. We are testing four attributes of the Minitel: its speed, information, comprehensibility and cost. The strength or importance of each of these attributes is determined using a scale from 1 for high importance to 3 for low importance. Each attribute can be evaluated using a scale such as the semantic differential, with 1 for a high evaluation through to 7 for a low one. The scores are then summed up to give a total attitudinal score, the lower the number meaning the more favourable the attitude. In the case of the Minitel, the following table could describe the responses of one individual:

Minitel Attributes	Importance (bi)	Evaluation (ai)	Product (bi x ai)
Speed	1	4	4
Information	2	5	10
Comprehensibility	3	3	9
Cost	1	1	1
	Attitude Score = 24		

The maximum score the product could have achieved here is 84, and with a score of 24 the consumer in question is rating it very highly, indicating speed and cost as the most important attributes.

Advantages and disadvantages

The main advantage of Fishbein's First Model is that it treats attitudes as sophisticated, multidimensional variables, which are weighted and affected by important attributes. The appreciation of the complicated nature of these variables has helped marketers to operate in a more informed way and to emphasise certain aspects of a product in order to improve its marketability. One of the main disadvantages is that a positive attitude does not necessarily mean that a consumer will buy the product in question. In the Minitel example above, a consumer may have a very positive attitude towards it after a public demonstration but may not have a phone. In many cases consumers do not have the money to buy goods towards which they have a positive attitude. This discrepancy between a consumer's attitudes towards products and his intention to buy led Fishbein to frame his extended model.

5.9.2 Fishbein's Extended Model (1975)

On the basis of criticisms of his first model, Fishbein reviewed his model and, with the help of Azjen, proposed his extended model. This states that a person's intentions to act are a function of how he perceives the product, what consequence it may lead to and the chance he thinks it has of achieving that consequence. In other words, the difference between the scales that would measure these variables and the ones used for Fishbein's earlier attitude model is that now the focus is on the *consequences* of purchase *behaviour* rather than the attributes of the object. This produces a function which describes the chance of the person's performing the act of buying the goods, as expressed in the following formula:

$$A\text{-act} = \sum_{i=1}^{n} b_i\, e_i$$

where:

A-act   =   the individual's perception of performing a particular act (e.g. buying a Minitel)

bi   =   the individual's perceived belief that performing the behaviour will lead to some consequence i

ei   =   the individual's evaluation of consequence i

n   =   the number of salient consequences involved.

Loudon and Della Butta (1993) represented the concept in this diagram:

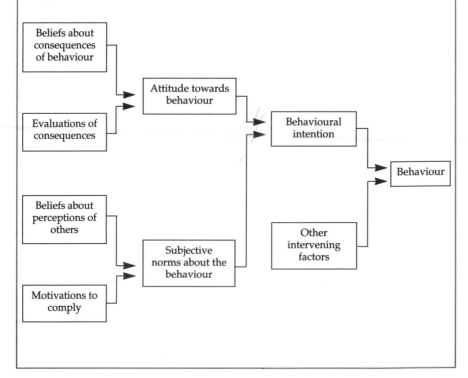

Advantages and disadvantages

The main criticism of this extended model is that it still does not predict whether a consumer will actually buy a particular product on the basis of his attitude, though it does give us a better picture of what he thinks of the product — especially because it examines not just how the consumer views the product, but also how he views the act of buying it.

5.10 ATTITUDE CHANGE

In previous sections we have noted how long-lasting and persistent attitudes are. The likelihood of changing a person's attitude is quite slim, given that — according to Katz (1960) — each attitude provides a function. He believed it was impossible to change an attitude until we first realised the function it served for the individual concerned.

It is difficult to alter attitudes and perhaps the only method available to politicians, marketers and others wishing to implement a change is through the communication process.

A simple model of the communication process demonstrates this point:

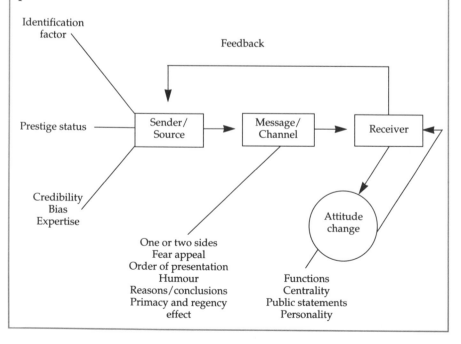

Source factors

Many factors influence the process of attitude change within the 'sender' variable, whether the sender is a company, a group or an individual. We review several of the major factors:

(a) **Credibility:** The higher the credibility (perceived by the receiver) the sender or source possesses, the greater the likelihood of attitude change.

(b) **Bias:** If the sender is perceived as being in any way biased towards the 'message', the receiver's orientation towards the sender decreases, leading to little if any attitude change.

(c) **Like or identify with receiver:** If the sender is liked or can be identified in any way with, and by, the receiver, attitude change may occur. Physical characteristics such as gender, age, attractiveness can influence receiver attitude.

(d) **Perceived expertise:** If the communicator is perceived as being expert or as possessing high qualifications to speak on the topic, influence may occur.

(e) **Prestige/Status:** More credibility is attached to a communicator if he is perceived to have status or prestige through either occupation, wealth or title. Frequently prestige and status are attributes conferred on individuals by society.

Message factors

If the communication procedure is viewed as a completely interactive process, it is important to understand message factors.

(a) **One/Two sides of message:** In general terms, presenting one side of the message is effective if the audience is already in agreement with the communicator. The message serves to reinforce views or beliefs. By presenting two sides of a message, there is an impression that a fair and objective handling of the message is being given. This is more effective if the audience is undecided. However, opinion tends to be divided on this matter. Recently the issue has centred on the educational level of the audience. If educated, audience members are regarded as being more perceptive, welcoming the opportunity to decide for themselves by being presented with a two-sided message. Those less well educated are said to appreciate the simplicity of a one-sided argument or message.

(b) **Order of presentation:** Where should the relevant and important parts of a message be placed to have the most impact? A general rule of thumb:

   (i) **beginning of the message** if there is a low level of audience interest

   (ii) **end of the message** if there is a high level of audience interest.

(c) **Primacy and recency effect:** In two-sided messages, is it better to present important parts of the communicator's stance first (primacy) or last (recency)? Again, opinions differ, but generally the last heard tends to be the best remembered.

(d) **Reasons/Conclusions:** In order to maximise audience favour, the message must fulfil a number of conditions:

   (i) address why they should listen

   (ii) use questions to generate involvement

   (iii) use concrete items rather than abstract terminology

   (iv) use familiar examples

   (v) draw conclusions for audience.

(e) **Fear/Humour appeals:** The use of message appeals is extremely important. Fear appeal centres on avoidance of social disapproval (e.g. use this deodorant if you don't want to be ostracised) and physical danger (decrease your alcohol intake to avoid drink driving). Humour appeal should be used selectively for two reasons: (a) it is a unique attribute and (b) frequently humour overpowers the product message.

Receiver factors

Here we concentrate on the audience or receiver variables and how these affect the communication process.

(a) **Personality:** Generally the more confident the receiver and the higher his self-esteem the less persuadable or in need of social approval he is. Attitude change may not occur for this type of receiver as his attitudes to life are well thought out.

(b) **Centrality:** The importance or the centrality of the attitude held by the receiver denotes whether change will occur. For example, the more central the attitude is to a receiver's value system, the less likely the attitude will be changed.

(c) **Public statements:** If the receiver has publicly stated his attitude towards a particular topic or object, this act alone will probably prevent attitude change.

(d) **Functions of attitudes:** As we noted earlier, whatever function or motivational base a particular attitude serves for the receiver, he will not change his attitude — however persuasive the communicator — unless the alternative provides a similar function, e.g. ego-defensive, value-expressive.

This chapter has shown how important an understanding of attitudes is in comprehending people's responses to the world around them, as well as demonstrating how complex and responsive to change they can be.

5.11 SUMMARY

1. Attitudes are learned predispositions to act in a favourable or unfavourable way towards an object or situation.
2. Attitudes fulfil four motivational bases or functions: adjustive, ego-defensive, value-expressive and knowledge.
3. We learn attitudes from a great variety of sources: family, peers, friends, culture, media and experience.
4. An attitude consists of three components: cognitive, affective and conative.
5. Attitudes and behaviour are linked but depend on a variety of interacting factors.
6. There are four principal scales for measuring attitudes: semantic differential, Thurstone, Likert and Guttman.
7. Consistency theories of attitudes (Balance, Cognitive Dissonance and Congruity) state that an individual will always act to regain mental consistency if disharmony exists.
8. Fishbein's Theory of Reasoned Action offers a more complex and sophisticated attitudinal model depicting the interaction of beliefs, values and knowledge bases.
9. Attitude change is difficult to achieve. The communication process, using sender, message and receiver variables, offers opportunities to attempt attitude change.

5.12 EXAM QUESTIONS

1. What are the variables involved in attitudinal change?
2. Why are the consistency theories of attitudes so called? (MII, 1992)
3. What is meant by Cognitive Dissonance and how can it affect people's behaviour? (MII, 1990)
4. Describe the main attitudinal scales, giving examples of areas in which each might be used.
5. What are the functions of attitudes?

Personality

6.1   INTRODUCTION

6.2   DEFINITION
       6.2.1 Nomothetic and idiographic
              approaches to personality theory

6.3   THEORIES AND THEORISTS
       6.3.1 Sigmund Freud
       6.3.2 Carl Gustav Jung
       6.3.3 Raymond Bernard Cattell
       6.3.4 Carl Rogers

6.4   SUMMARY

6.5   EXAM QUESTIONS

Learning Objectives

After studying this chapter you should be able to:

— *Present an informed and comprehensive opinion on the nature of personality*
— *Understand the contributions of Sigmund Freud in the field of the unconscious*
— *Identify Jung's psychological types within personality development*
— *Describe Cattell's personality theory in terms of traits*
— *Understand Carl Rogers' 'nurturing' approach to personality.*

6.1 INTRODUCTION

Personality is a multidimensional concept. Most people use the term 'personality' in a descriptive way, e.g. 'she has a warm, friendly personality', but psychologically speaking this is incorrect. Behavioural scientists speak of personality in broader terms, stressing the interaction of a number of processes, such as attitudes, motives and values. It is amazing that despite the years of research the topic has engendered, no one agreed universal definition has emerged. Scientists broadly agree on one fact, however: one should view personality in terms of the *totality* of the person rather than focusing on specific attributes.

A knowledge of personality theories provides us with a basic understanding of a person's orientation, whether towards a product (consumers), an employer (work attitude) or social issues. This chapter begins with the questions posed by researchers so that we see the parameters used for a definition of personality. Next, two orientations of study are introduced: the notion that personality is inherent and fixed; and the contrary, that it develops and changes. Finally, we examine four important personality theorists: Freud, Jung, Cattell and Rogers.

6.2 DEFINITION

Despite the large number of differing theories, researchers have found common ground in the questions that should be asked when seeking to arrive at a definition. For example:

(a) What is personality?

(b) What variables go into making up personality, and are they permanent or transient?

(c) Is our personality already formed when we are born or are we completely shaped by the environment, or is it a mixture of both?

(d) How can one measure, by means of tests, a person's personality?

(e) How accurate are these tests?

(f) How much of a person's true personality does he show to the outside world?

(g) To what extent can we ever know our own personalities?

(h) Is our behaviour unique or is personality common to all of us as human beings?

The following theories address these questions in varying ways, each presenting a different perspective on personality. The definition of personality we propose is from Gross (1992): 'those relatively stable and enduring aspects of individuals which distinguish them from other people, making them unique, but which at the same time permit a comparison between individuals'.

6.2.1 Nomothetic and idiographic approaches to personality theory

The main division in approaches to personality research is between (a) those who believe personality comprises permanent traits or characteristics, and (b) those who advocate studying unique individuals, so as to arrive at an overall understanding of personality in general.

(a) Raymond Cattell belongs to the first category. He believes our personalities are composed of factors which are relatively permanent and which can be measured and analysed by psychometric tests. The interpretation of personality is made more accurate, according to Cattell, by identifying and measuring relevant traits. This is known as the **nomothetic** approach.

(b) The second main approach, the **idiographic**, states that because we are unique, we each display personality characteristics reflecting our own idiosyncratic characters. This view is espoused by the psychoanalytic/psychodynamic theorists such as Freud and Jung, and humanistic psychologists such as Maslow and Rogers. These theorists suggest that rather than analysing individual traits, and trying to 'add together' a personality, we must look at the expression of a personality in a person's behaviour. Further, they would say that one's personality can change through psychoanalysis, the intervention of other professionals, and self-reflection.

6.3 THEORIES AND THEORISTS

6.3.1 Sigmund Freud

The first of the major theorists on personality, Sigmund Freud (1856–1939) is perhaps the most famous psychologist/psychiatrist/psychoanalyst to have contributed to an understanding of the human mind. For one who wrote so extensively and has been so widely translated, he is also one of the most misunderstood writers in the field of psychology.

How often do we say that someone has committed a Freudian slip, without having been formally introduced to this term and without really understanding what it means? Many of his phrases and ideas have been assumed into common usage without being properly put in context. Freud was a writer of his time, concerned primarily with sexually repressed patients in Vienna at the turn of the century. We may take it for granted today that each of us has a subconscious mind, but such a fact was unknown when Freud began his work as a psychiatrist.

Personality, according to Freud, is the result of psychic energy which finds expression through three strong, interacting mental forces: the **Id**, the **Ego**, and the **Super-Ego**.

The Id, the deepest and strongest source of psychic energy, works solely on the 'Pleasure Principle' of immediate and total satisfaction of its needs, regardless of the consequences. It exists to avoid discomfort and pain and to accrue only pleasure. It operates on a subjective and subconscious level, tending not to recognise objective reality or to realise that some desires are socially unacceptable, e.g. aggressiveness.

The Ego, working on the 'Reality Principle', deals with the outside world, attempting to control the Id by channelling psychic energy into socially acceptable and realistic behaviours. The Ego acts as a mediator of psychic energy, helping individuals to deal realistically with their environment. It is the only one of the three to operate on a conscious level.

The Super-Ego, working on the 'Moral Principle', is regarded as the conscience of the individual. It attempts to control the Id's basic instincts (which are frequently socially unacceptable) whilst influencing the Ego in moral rather than realistic actions. The Super-Ego strives for the ideal. Like the Id it is subconscious in nature.

To give a simple example of the three forces at work: the Id demands chocolate now (pleasure), the Super-Ego (conscience) tells us dinner is ready and not to spoil our appetite whilst the Ego (reality) suggests we have the chocolate as dessert.

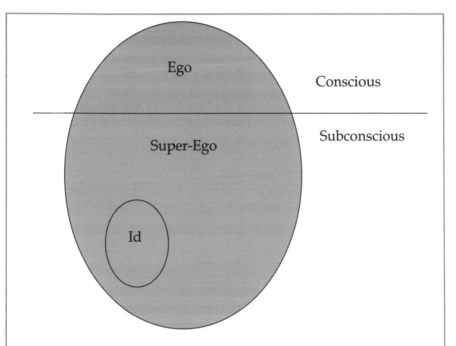

The structure of the conscious and subconscious mind, according to Freud

Stages of development

Personality is defined by the interaction of Id, Ego and Super-Ego, and their handling of psychic energy or tension. How our personality actually develops, according to Freud, is through a psychosexual process, consisting of five stages. The presence of the Id, Ego and Super-Ego is constant throughout our developmental stages, but they really begin operating when we reach maturity. A young infant, for example, tends to be all 'Id', demanding constant satisfaction, whilst a child of eight to ten years begins to enter the 'age of reason' and of moral considerations (Super-Ego).

The psychosexual developmental process comprises five stages, each possessing physical importance for the infant or child. Progress through each stage is of utmost importance in terms of adult behaviour in later years. Freud pointed out that we do not necessarily pass peaceably through these stages, nor is there a rigid time structure. Those who fail, or become stuck, in any one stage tend to exhibit behavioural problems in adulthood.

The main developmental stages Freud defined as follows:

Stage	Age	Characteristics	Adult Behavioural Problems
1. Oral	0–1	Concerned with senses, of which mouth is the most sensitive. Can turn out to be orally incorporating or orally expulsive.	e.g. silent or chatterbox
2. Anal	1–2	Concerned with controlling its defecation. May turn out to be anally retentive or anally expulsive	e.g. tight-fisted or very generous
3. Phallic	2–5	Has to cope with resolving its Oedipus or Electra complex, and may learn to identify with same-sex parent.	e.g. confused sexual orientation
4. Latency	5–12	Sexual thoughts or behaviour are put into the subconscious. Also, Super-Ego and Id go into the subconscious.	e.g. ability to take part in ordinary life
5. Genital	12 on	In this stage the person reaches mature adult sexuality.	

1. **Oral stage:** The child is concerned exclusively with its physical senses, the mouth being the most sensitive. This can carry over into later life in terms of an adult being either orally incorporating (by which he tries to acquire knowledge or collect things) or orally expulsive (which means he becomes very sarcastic or argumentative). In a marketing context, marketers may seek to satisfy the needs of oral incorporators by trying to sell them goods which appeal to their desire

for knowledge, such as educational courses, books or even encyclopedias. The needs of orally expulsive consumers may be satisfied by such things as commercial radio phone-ins or particular types of video programmes.

2. **Anal stage:** The child — through its parents and its toilet training — learns to control its defecation. In complying with its parents' wishes, the child progresses normally through this stage. Alternatively, he can be anally retentive or anally expulsive. In either case the child may behave in this way to displease its parents or to establish its own independence. With anal retentiveness the child may turn out to be excessively stubborn or excessively concerned with detail, order or cleanliness. A marketer could appeal to this type of person with products which promote cleanliness and order, such as detergents and filing systems. With anal expulsiveness the child may develop into an adult who is disorderly, destructive or cruel. Marketers could target them with products emphasising individuality and nonconformism.

3. **Phallic stage:** The child is highly concerned with its genitals. The Oedipus complex (for a male child) and the Electra complex (for a female child) exists here. These are mechanisms by which the child learns to resolve (in most cases) its feelings of sexual attraction towards its parent of the opposite sex, ultimately identifying with the parent of the same sex.

4. **Latency stage:** Between the end of the phallic stage and the beginning of the final stage, there is the latency period (between the ages of five and twelve) where feelings and actions already described are put into the subconscious at the age of five, to reappear at the age of twelve. The difference is that, at the age of twelve, the adolescent is now developing sexual feelings and a concern for others in his environment, whereas previously he was self-centred. Marketers frequently target this stage by emphasising sex role stereotypes to adolescents, teenagers or even adults who wish to identify with the fashion and behavioural habits of their own sex. The converse can also be true, and marketers may wish to target those who are not satisfied with the fashion norms which currently exist.

5. **Genital stage:** Through this the child reaches mature adult sexuality. Marketers would target those who see themselves as sensible, mature adults wanting to live up to the responsibilities of life.

Defence mechanisms

The peaceful channelling of psychic energy by the three personality components (Id, Ego and Super-Ego) is more often than not achieved. However, there are occasions when the Ego (Reality Principle) fails as a mediator, causing tremendous psychic tension, which in turn results in an unresolved situation. Rather than suffer this tension, the individual devises 'defence mechanisms'. These are unconsciously determined techniques brought into existence in order to deal with the state of tension. A great number exist, including:

Fixation: In an effort to avoid new situations with their concomitant challenges and insecurities, individuals cling to what is familiar. Individuals fixate in what to them is a familiar, tried and tested routine, e.g. instead of progressing to a more challenging and responsible role, an employee may remain overqualified in his present job.

Projection: In order to eliminate anxiety or tension-filled emotions from our own minds, we project such states onto others, e.g. we project feelings of insecurity onto others rather than express them ourselves.

Repression: We deliberately forget threatening information in order to cope with the present situation, e.g. denying the existence of upsetting knowledge.

Regression: We regress or return to behaviours more suitable to earlier stages of development, because of an inability to cope with the present situation, e.g. tantrums.

Although Freud's theory has had profound effects on later psychological theorists, a number of criticisms have been levelled at his work:

(a) It is a very sexually orientated theory, with the notions of self-concept and self-esteem virtually dismissed.

(b) Freud's theory is deterministic in the sense that it pays little heed to external factors — he believed that the process begins at birth and continues regardless of experiences. Personality, for Freud, is determined by the age of five.

(c) The theory dismisses cultural, or societal, influences regardless of societal norms, values and institutions. Freud held that all personalities develop in this particular way, i.e. without social or cultural influence.

(d) He dismisses individual differences, such as attitudes, motives, the ability to empathise.

(e) The theory is unscientific. His research consisted of case-studies and interviews; no measurement, definitions or data were given.

These are the main aspects of Freud's theories. For a fuller exposition of his work, see the references for this chapter. Outside the clinical sphere, Freud's ideas are used by some in marketing to segment the market for particular products, this segmentation being called psychographics.

6.3.2 Carl Gustav Jung

Jung (1875–1961), at one stage a colleague of Freud's, is also a proponent of the psychodynamic view of personality. His conception of personality is of a dynamic psyche, self-regulating and in constant movement, with energy flowing between two opposing poles. When energy flows to the progression pole the individual is concerned with active adaptation to his environment, while regression energy manifests itself in the satisfying of unconscious needs. In this idea of opposites, Jung focused on the concept of people constantly trying to adapt to their own and society's needs. He placed great emphasis on cultural and spiritual contributions to personality development, noting that the inner or psychic process is equal in value to the environmental or outer process.

Jung's concept of personality expresses itself in the notion of psychological types, i.e. the flow of energy results in either outward orientation or inward orientation — again the opposites.

Jung discerned eight basic personality types: four main types (detailed below), each with two subdivisions — introversion and extroversion. The first two functions Jung categorised as rational (i.e. thinking and feeling) and the latter two as non-rational (i.e. sensing and intuiting).

	Introversion	*Extroversion*
1. Thinking (intellectual)	Likely to direct their mental energies towards themselves	Likely to direct their mental energies towards others
2. Feeling (evaluative)	More likely to have reflective and self-conscious feelings	Emotions are more likely to include others
3. Sensing (senses)	Those who are aware of the world around but whose activities are more inwardly directed, e.g. painters	Sensitive to the outside world but directed towards others in their activities, e.g. performing artists
4. Intuiting (intuitive)	Subconscious understanding of the world, directed inwards	Subconscious understanding of the world, directed towards others

The functions of Jung's personality theory

1. **Thinking function** (our intellectual function): 'Thinking' people react to situations analytically and are very conscious of the implications of their actions for themselves and for others. Jung believed there were both introverted and extroverted thinking types, the difference being that the former were more likely to direct mental energies towards their own activities whereas the latter were more likely to direct their energies towards interaction with others. An example of an introverted thinking type might be a reclusive university professor, and an extroverted thinking type an outgoing, enthusiastic teacher.

2. **Feeling function** (our evaluative function, by which we accept or reject things on the basis of positive or negative impulses): 'Feeling' people react to situations in terms of emotions such as friendliness, joy or even suspicion. The introverted types are more likely to have reflective, self-conscious feelings, whereas the extroverted types are more likely to embrace others and direct their energies/feelings outwards.

3. **Sensing function** (our senses — smell, touch, taste, sight, etc.): This might be termed the artistic function as it includes those who are highly aware of the world around them. Simple examples of the introverted and extroverted types might be a novelist or poet (who have to withdraw by the very nature of their work) and an actor or street performer (usually a very outgoing expressive type).

4. **Intuiting function** (our subconscious perception of our world, by which we may have a 'hunch' about something): 'Intuitive' people use empathy as a basis for communication, e.g. in the way a psychologist might seek to understand a patient. Once again, the introverted types direct this understanding towards themselves whilst the extroverted types direct it towards other people.

Jung believed that our personalities develop as a function of interaction with our physical, mental and cultural environments. Although he stipulated his eight personality types, he recognised that they were not mutually exclusive.

6.3.3 Raymond Bernard Cattell

Cattell (1905–) did not place emphasis on the structure of the conscious and subconscious mind. Instead, he sought to understand personality by analysing what he believed were the roots of our personalities — what he called traits. He defined a trait as 'an inferred mental structure that accounts for the consistency of observed behaviours'. He divided traits into two categories: 'surface' and 'source' traits, and saw personality as a function of the interaction, or balance, between the two.

Surface traits are those which are usually readily apparent in a particular individual, e.g. Mary is vivacious, friendly and generally outgoing. **Source traits** are harder to discern. Cattell described them as combinations of not readily apparent parts of a person's make-up which emerge only when we subject these personality constituents to close mathematical analysis. According to him, source traits interact to produce surface traits — which in turn lead to particular behaviours.

The importance of source traits was highlighted by Cattell when he introduced a further categorisation system: (a) **constitutional** and (b) **environmental mould**. Constitutional source traits we are born with and they remain the same throughout our lives. Environmental source traits are dynamic (i.e. goal-orientated), responding to changes within our environment. The latter are again divided: firstly, by 'ability', which determines the effectiveness of an individual's efforts to achieve a certain goal; secondly, by 'temperament', which is the how, at what speed and at what energy level an individual attempts a goal. This can be seen in the following diagram:

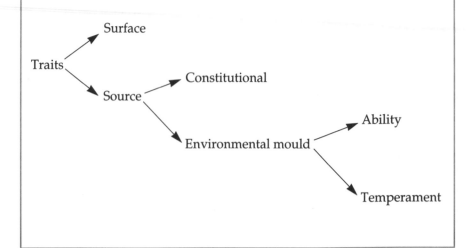

The structure of Cattell's personality theory

Cattell sought to provide a realistic grounding for his theory of
personality structure. He devised a personality questionnaire
(16pf) which attempted to measure personality. The 16pf
(personality factors) consisted of the traits Cattell felt made up an
individual's personality.

	Letter Symbol and Factor Name	
Outgoing	A (Affectia–Sizia)	Reserved
More intelligent	B (Intelligence)	Less intelligent
Stable	C (Ego strength)	Emotional
Assertive	E (Dominance–Submissiveness)	Humble
Happy-go-lucky	F (Surgency–Desurgency)	Sober
Conscientious	G (Super-Ego strength)	Expedient
Bold	H (Parmia–Threctia)	Shy
Tender-minded	I (Premsia–Harria)	Tough-minded
Suspicious	L (Protension–Alaxia)	Trusting
Imaginative	M (Autia–Praxernia)	Practical
Shrewd	N (Shrewdness–Artlessness)	Forthright
Apprehensive	O (Guilt-proneness–Assurance)	Placid
Experimenting	Q1 (Radicalism–Conservatism)	Traditional
Self-sufficient	Q2 (Self-sufficiency–Group adherence)	Group-tied
Controlled	Q3 (High self-concept–Low integration)	Casual
Tense	Q4 (Ergic tension)	Relaxed

The sixteen factors in Cattell's 16pf

Cattell espoused the use of mathematical techniques in personality
research. His 16pf is analysed through factor analysis — a
mathematical procedure devised to tease out what source and
surface traits are inherent in the questionnaire respondent.

Cattell tackles the issues in the 'nature and nurture' debate, in that he
believes that we are born with traits which stay with us throughout
our lives (i.e. constitutional source traits) but also possess traits
which develop and change in response to the conditions around us
(i.e. environmental mould source traits). It is the former, he states,
which are predominant in the forming of personality.

Evaluation

Cattell's theories have been used a great deal in the business world. The 16pf is a very versatile tool in personnel selection, in that it can easily categorise individuals into different types and thus determine whether they are suitable for the job in question. The 16pf has also found uses in the educational and marketing fields. Yet there are many criticisms of Cattell's theories. For example, his structuring of personality theory is within the confines of mathematical techniques and so could be considered not to pick up the subtleties and irrationalities of human behaviour. His approach to theorising attempts scientific methodology but pays little heed to the concept of the unconscious, or the idea of the self.

Nevertheless, his work aims to clarify the theory of personality in unambiguous terms, introducing the precision of an empirical approach.

6.3.4 Carl Rogers

A proponent of the 'Nurturing'/'Self-Concept' development of personality, Rogers (1902–89) opposes the idea that personality is structured. His theory of personality was developed from clinical experience in his famous 'person-centred psychotherapy'. Rogers believes that people are naturally orientated towards positive actions and growth. His work with patients highlighted two constructs, or components, of personality:

(a) **Organism:** the physical and psychological functioning of the individual, incorporating the totality of conscious and unconscious experiences.

(b) **Self-Concept:** comprising the 'I' of one's own perceptions and characteristics, and the 'me' in relation to others. Embedded within this component is the notion of an ideal self (what I strive or would like to achieve), and the actual self (the actual me, as I now am).

In terms of personality development, Rogers believes that both components are affected by our experiences, and our relationships with others. If we experience what he referred to as 'unconditional acceptance', firstly from our parents, then from important others throughout our lives, we feel secure in ourselves. Personality development for Rogers is a process where the notions of the organism and the self are in harmony. Problems arise when this unconditional acceptance is transformed into 'conditional acceptance', and individuals experience **incongruency** or **denial**.

Incongruency manifests itself in an upset between the organism and the self. According to Rogers, a healing can take place if true acceptance is given and the individual feels secure. It is interesting to note that he considers personality a continuing process of valuing, rather than — as our previous theorists do — a system.

His theory has promoted the idea of the 'self' within personality theory, giving rise to recognition within scientific circles of the therapeutic process. He has attempted measurement through self-reports, interviews and group work in order to bring clarity to a complex topic. His theory ignores the unconscious element within personality development and is often regarded as too optimistic and simplistic in that he deems it possible to heal and make whole all people regardless of personality disorders. The psychoanalytic theorists disagree totally.

Our examination of four very different approaches to personality development demonstrates the complexity of the concept. The questions asked include: whether it is expressed through behaviour or through feelings; whether it consists of traits; whether it is moulded through the environment and experience. Does the unconscious play as big a part as Freud would have us believe, or is it as clear-cut as Cattell suggests? Whatever approach or orientation is adopted it is important to realise that no one theorist provides the answer. Personality consists of many facets. Our knowledge of personality theory can offer only *suggestions* as to why people behave as they do.

6.4 SUMMARY

1. Personality is difficult to define but generally consists of relatively stable and enduring aspects.
2. Freud suggests that personality is made up of three components: the Id, the Ego and the Super-Ego, and is developed within five stages.
3. Jung places more emphasis on the cultural and social development of personality and suggests that it is expressed through four personality types: thinking, feeling, sensing and intuiting.
4. Cattell believes that personality comprises surface and source traits whose interaction produces a personality type. He invented the 16pf test, a questionnaire attempting personality measurement.
5. Rogers sees personality as a developmental process between the self and the organism, and believes that positive and unconditional acceptance leads to a positive and happy personality.

6.5 EXAM QUESTIONS

1. Show how the Self-Concept Theory differs from other personality theories. (MII, 1992)
2. Critically examine Trait Theory as an explanation of human personality. (MII, 1991)
3. Explain the ways in which Freud's and Jung's psychoanalytic theories are similar, and how each differs from the other.
4. 'Nomothetic and idiographic theories are, by their very nature, incompatible.' Discuss.
5. 'Where Cattell is explicit and precise, Freud is implicit and unclear.' Discuss.

Groups

7.1   INTRODUCTION

7.2   GROUPS
      7.2.1 What is a group?
      7.2.2 Reasons for joining a group

7.3   CATEGORISATIONS OF GROUPS
      7.3.1 Categorisations
      7.3.2 Reference group

7.4   GROUP STRUCTURE
      7.4.1 Cohesiveness
      7.4.2 Status
      7.4.3 Roles
      7.4.4 Norms
      7.4.5 Communication
      7.4.6 Size

7.5   GROUP DEVELOPMENT
      7.5.1 How groups develop
      7.5.2 Stages of group development

7.6   GROUP POWER
      7.6.1 Power
      7.6.2 Reasons for conforming
      7.6.3 Research in conformity
      7.6.4 Hawthorne Studies

7.7   SUMMARY

7.8   EXAM QUESTIONS

Learning Objectives

After studying this chapter you should be able to:

— *Understand what is meant by a group and some of the reasons why people join groups*
— *Explain the different categories of groups*
— *Identify the nature of group structure, its processes and stages of development*
— *Discuss how groups exert power over members' behaviour*
— *Describe the Hawthorne Studies.*

7.1 INTRODUCTION

Studying individuals together, i.e. in a group, one might expect to be relatively simple — in that it is a collection of individuals. This assumption is incorrect. Once individuals begin interacting and interrelating, a subtle and pervasive force is at work. However, as Hackman and Morris (1975) suggest, while 'something important happens in group interaction . . . there is little agreement about what that "something" is'.

Our lives are made up of a great many groups: family, peers, social and work, to name but a few. Each possesses rules and regulates our behaviour. In this chapter we examine many group issues: why and how they develop, why people join, what types of groups exist. Perhaps one of the most important questions addressed is why groups are so influential.

From an organisational viewpoint, management may wish to harness what is referred to as 'synergy', the collective output of a group stimulated by member interaction. Work groups are usually created by management in order to perform particular tasks or functions, but they sometimes emerge naturally as a consequence of the division of labour. Management must be aware of group dynamic concepts — that is, the force operating within the group — in order to keep control and motivate employees.

From a marketing viewpoint, the concept of group formation and membership has tremendous implications. Work and social groups influence consumer-related attitudes and activities. Frequently, consumers are unaware that they look to others for direction as to which products to buy. Indeed, these 'others' are also unaware that they serve as a consumption-related model, or reference group, to use the correct terminology.

In everyday life, group membership influences social involvement. Being a member of a particular group can fulfil many psychological needs, such as security, esteem, or just companionship. A knowledge of group dynamics offers insight into our own behaviour and that of others.

We begin by defining a group and discussing the varied reasons people have for joining. We next examine the various categorisations, along with the structure and development of groups. Finally, we study the power of a group and how it may influence individual behaviour.

7.2 GROUPS

7.2.1 What is a group?

A group is any number of people who:

(a) interact with each other

(b) are psychologically aware of each other

(c) perceive themselves to be a group.

In other words, they have a collective identity, a sense of relatedness as a result of interaction with each other. All three of the above conditions must be met in order for a collection of people to call itself a group.

Frequently, a cinema queue or bus queue is referred to as a group, purely because the people happen to be in close proximity. This is psychologically incorrect. Such collections are merely aggregates of people.

It is important to understand that the behaviour of individuals both affects and is affected by the group: a two-way relationship exists.

7.2.2 Reasons for joining a group

People have many different reasons for joining groups. We join to fulfil a need (or needs). Indeed, by joining one group, several needs can be served at once. In general, we join for the following reasons:

(a) **Security:** We feel secure if we belong to a group. The maxim 'safety in numbers' highlights this fact. Whether facing a new situation or a new challenge, being part of a group reduces anxiety. Take, for example, joining an already established social club. It would be normal to feel awkward and embarrassed, experiencing that 'everyone knows everyone else' sensation. If, on the other hand, we join on a 'new members' night, we immediately feel less anxious — purely because we are one of the crowd. We feel secure because of the 'protection' offered by the group.

(b) **Affiliation:** The need for companionship or the presence of other people centres on this 'affiliation' need. Frequently, a group is a source of personal value to an individual because it satisfies the need for being in the company of others. Widows' Associations, for example, attempt to fulfil the affiliation need by replacing lost companionship. Widows join, not particularly for activities or interests, but purely to be with other people.

(c) **Social identity:** People see themselves as psychologically intertwined with a group — that is, the group can often reflect our self-image. Groups as diverse as Young Mums & Toddlers Groups and Vincent de Paul help us to establish a sense of identity with like-minded people. The group 'grounds' us, providing both security and a sense of self. We feel we belong. Work, interest and friendship groups all offer a sense of identity.

(d) **Goals:** When an individual recognises the mutuality of his own goals with those of a particular group, he often responds by joining. The group's power is frequently greater than the individual's, thus it makes sense for them to join forces. Where this is the case, the individual tends to be prepared to offer both commitment and time. Take, for example, the Neighbourhood Watch Scheme, which plays an integral role in today's housing areas. Individual and group goals are similar — to prevent crime — but how much more powerful is the combined effort?

(e) **Activities:** We sometimes join a group purely because its activities offer us satisfaction. In sports clubs, for instance, many members want only the enjoyment of playing the sport or keeping fit. Likewise with night classes, people join because they wish to participate in the activity and not necessarily to become experts.

(f) **Interpersonal attraction:** This may be the most obvious of reasons for joining a group — because of the attractiveness of its members. There are three influencing factors:

   (i) perceived ability of the group

   (ii) perceived status of the group

   (iii) similarity in attitudes, beliefs and values.

There are other reasons for joining groups, such as proximity, physical attractiveness, race and economic self-interest. However, whatever our reasons (often unconscious), we seek fulfilment within the group structure. In return, there is a trade-off: we must obey the group. This is one of the most important aspects of group psychology, examined later in the chapter.

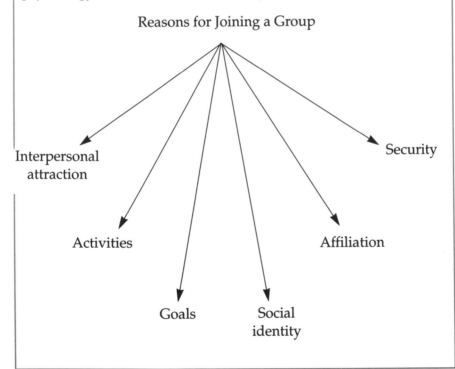

Reasons for Joining a Group

Interpersonal attraction

Security

Activities

Affiliation

Goals

Social identity

7.3 CATEGORISATIONS OF GROUPS

It would be almost impossible to function in society without belonging to a group. They exist everywhere: family, friends, work, socially. It is not until we stop and think about it that we realise just how many groups we belong to and are influenced by in our lives. Groups tend to differ in purpose and size and it is this differentiation which enables us to categorise or classify them.

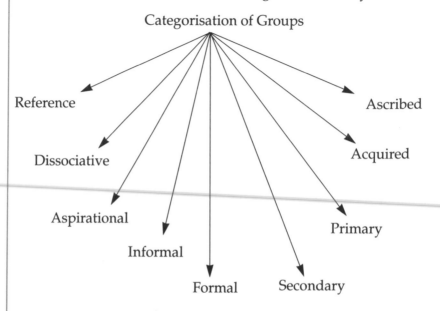

7.3.1 Categorisations

In general, the following categorisations exist:

(a) **Ascribed:** Membership is non-voluntary, we do not have a choice in the matter, e.g. family, school class, nationalities.

(b) **Acquired:** Membership is voluntary, we actively seek to belong, e.g. sports, social clubs.

(c) **Primary:** Small, intimate group with member communication and interaction on a one-to-one basis, e.g. study group, family, marketing team.

(d) **Secondary:** Large group; less continuous interaction than in Primary Group but group identity sufficiently present. Main distinction between Primary and Secondary Groups is the importance and frequency of interaction, e.g. head office is a secondary group to a regional office.

(e) **Formal groups:** Consciously created by management to meet the needs of the organisation with clear group structure, well-defined tasks and predetermined working procedures. Formal groups are characterised by a high management involvement in all aspects of group activities, e.g. special task force, committee, government body.

(f) **Informal:** Established by its members, socially active and consisting of friendship/interest groups. Management must recognise the importance of informal group structure because frequently these groups exercise strong control over their members, e.g. social groups of friends.

(g) **Aspirational:** An individual's perception of a group causes him to want or aspire to join, for a variety of reasons, e.g. perceived status. Such aspirational groups can have a profound influence on a non-member's behaviour because of his strong desire to join the group, e.g. local yacht or golf club.

(h) **Dissociative:** Works in reverse to the above and has a negative influence. Individuals avoid being identified with such groups, e.g. drug-takers, joy-riders.

We can be members of any number of such groups, adapting relatively easily to their respective rules and regulations. There is, however, one more important categorisation we must examine, that of the reference group.

7.3.2 Reference group

A reference group or groups are those an individual uses, or refers to, in determining his judgments, beliefs and behaviour. Our first reference group is the family, from which we adopt values, judgments and attitudes. Other reference groups follow: schoolfriends, peers, work associates. In fact, any of the above group categorisations may act as a reference group.

Reference groups often determine an individual's behaviour, in the sense that they:

(a) **provide comparisons:** individuals attempt to match and emulate reference group behaviour

(b) **provide guidelines:** individuals perceive and adopt rules that govern members' behaviour.

The concept of a reference group is used widely in marketing. It is generally acknowledged that consumers accept reference group influence because of the perceived benefits in doing so, i.e. status and identity (Loudon and Della Butta, 1993).

With so many categorisations, one wonders if all groups are structured in the same way. Is there a difference in make-up between, say, an informal group and a reference group? Group structure may differ in cohesiveness (staying-power) or status (power levels), but it always refers to the way in which its members relate to each other.

7.4 GROUP STRUCTURE

Group structure may be defined in terms of a relatively stable pattern of relationships among particular aspects of a group. These aspects, or differentiated elements, consist of cohesiveness, status, roles, norms, communication and size.

In other words, group structure refers to members behaving in a consistent and agreed manner in relation to the above elements, providing the stability or consistency the group needs in order to survive. We examine these elements to understand how each contributes towards a picture of a group.

7.4.1 Cohesiveness

This refers to the motivation of members to remain in the group. It encourages conformity, stability and a sharing of activities. Group cohesiveness results from 'forces acting on the members to remain in the group' (Festinger, 1950) and includes:

(a) **Interaction of members:** The more frequently people meet, the more they get to know each other and the more they perceive themselves as a group. This in turn eases communication among members and fosters group identity.

(b) **Goals and tasks:** If tasks and objectives are clear, unambiguous and relevant, members will feel a greater sense of motivation and achievement.

(c) **Mature development of group:** The longer the group has been in existence, the more likely members are prepared to continue their association with, and participation in, it.

(d) **Homogeneity:** The more similar members are in areas such as attitudes, motivations, education, status, the more they will share common perspectives and group goals.

(e) **Nature of external environment:** If individuals perceive their environment as hostile, a group offering protection will be welcomed and loyalty and commitment assigned.

7.4.2 Status

This refers to the assigning of a power level to an individual, e.g. chairperson, treasurer. The assigning of status within a group serves three important functions:

(a) **Motivation:** Status provides reward/incentive basis for performance or achievement, e.g. an employee may be encouraged to perform particularly well if a promotion such as 'head buyer' is on offer.

(b) **Identification:** Status provides useful cues for acceptable behaviour towards hierarchical relationships. It is useful in a job to know the chain of authority because most of us tend to alter and/or adapt our behaviour towards a work colleague in accordance with the position he holds.

(c) **Stability:** Status provides continuity in areas such as:

(i) **authority patterns:** it is a steadying influence when we know where authority lies

(ii) **role relationships:** we know how to act and respond to various colleagues

(iii) **interpersonal relationships:** we get to know and respond to people in their particular roles.

These three functions provide individuals with a consistent and unambiguous knowledge of group hierarchy. A question often asked is 'Is there status in informal social groups?' The answer is yes. Despite an informal group's lack of a definite structure or goal-directed behaviour, leaders still emerge (see 7.6.4) and a rather more subtle status hierarchy operates. For example, status may take the form of wealth, occupation or popularity. A group, whether formal or informal, always possesses hierarchy.

7.4.3 Roles

This refers to the part an individual plays or adopts in a group. A 'role' is basically a self-contained pattern of behaviour. Each role, whether leader or 'back-up', has its own pattern of behavioural expectations imposed by society. A mother may perceive her role as nurturing, encouraging and sympathetic. A supervisor may perceive his role as motivational, administrative and organisational. Whatever the role, an individual perceives and enacts role expectations with varying degrees of success.

Within organisational life, roles may be divided into three general areas:

(a) **Task:** Where the role focuses on task-related activities, ensuring that the group achieves its goals and maintains its schedule, e.g. the role occupied by the chairperson of a meeting.

(b) **Relations:** Where the role focuses on social relationships within the group in order to promote:

(i) harmony

(ii) welfare

(iii) cohesiveness.

This role attempts to promote a positive, rewarding atmosphere concerned more with members' feelings than with the task in hand, e.g. personnel officer or counsellor in a company.

(c) **Self-Orientation:** Where the role emphasises the specific needs/ goals of an individual, frequently at the expense of the group. It is often referred to as a group member having a 'hidden agenda'. In other words, the member possesses ulterior motives and does not fully participate within the group work ethos, e.g. a business person using a voluntary group to enhance his company's performance.

Within the context of defining 'roles', two further points are important:

(i) **Role ambiguity** refers to the uncertainty of an individual as to

(1) the exact nature of the job/role he has to perform, and

(2) others' expectations of the same role.

This can cause stress, insecurity and loss of self-confidence. It is extremely important that role requirements are explicit and unambiguously stated, making it easier for individuals to conform.

(ii) **Role conflict** occurs when expectations about an individual's role in the group contradict each other:

(1) Inter-role conflict occurs when an individual experiences conflict between two or more roles, e.g. the difficulties in trying to be both a boss and a friend to a work colleague.

(2) Intra-role conflict occurs when an individual receives contradictory messages concerning the same role, e.g. the difficulties for shop assistants when the boss marks their authority limit yet customers challenge them to take more responsibility.

How an individual perceives and carries out his role in the group has important implications for its overall functioning.

7.4.4 Norms

This refers to a standard against which the appropriateness of behaviour is measured. Two norms in our society are that (i) we go about fully clothed and (ii) we use knives and forks to eat our food. A norm is the expected behaviour in a certain setting.

Groups supply norms for their members for the following reasons:

(a) they provide an agenda for acceptable/unacceptable behaviour

(b) they provide roles for members in order to reduce confusion/ambiguity

(c) they provide for group survival — if deviant behaviour threatens the smooth flow of performance, the group will isolate or reject such deviancy

(d) they provide identification for members.

Pressures to conform to group norms are powerful determinants of group behaviour. In short, norms act as regulatory mechanisms. As these emerge, individuals begin to behave according to how they feel other group members expect them to behave. The acceptance of norms by a group member facilitates integration into the group and is taken as a signal that the individual concerned is committed to the group.

An academic study of the emergence of a group norm was carried out by Muzafer Sherif's Auto-Kinetic Effect experiment (Sherif and Sherif, 1969). He demonstrated how three individuals' different opinions converged as they gave repeated public estimates (over a four-day period) of the apparent movement of a point of light within a darkened room. The Auto-Kinetic Effect creates a perceptual illusion in which a light giving the appearance of movement is in fact stationary. Individuals' opinions differed widely on Day 1 of the experiment; Day 2 and Day 3 saw a moving closer together of opinions. Sherif postulated that this was because they heard each other's public statements and began to (a) doubt their own perceptions, and (b) agree with their fellows because of covert pressure. Day 4 saw a total convergence — the group of three had established a group 'norm', and felt satisfied they had seen the same thing.

7.4.5 Communication

This refers to the process of information being given in order to initiate/complete goal behaviours. There are two general modes of communication within groups:

Centralised: Information is channelled through one person with other group members having little or no interaction. Progress or regression on tasks is the responsibility of one person.

Decentralised: Information is free-flowing; group members are at liberty to cross lines of authority in order to accomplish goals.

The task in hand tends to dictate the communication mode. Where tasks are functional, centralisation is favoured. The more creative the task the more likely that communication is decentralised. For example, jobs that are basically straightforward can be standardised with communication one-directional. Jobs demanding creativity require a free flow of information and communication, so that ideas and messages can be shared and discussed.

7.4.6 Size

This refers to the number of group members. This variable can have an important effect not only on performance but also on interaction.

Generally, the smaller the group the more frequent the communication and interaction between members. Goal accomplishment tends to be reached very quickly with more member accountability. Small groups are usually less formal than larger groups and possess an ease of functioning. Larger groups, however, tend to have a higher generation of ideas, use of more resources and a larger expertise/skill base. It is true that there may be a more formalised communication pattern which in turn may inhibit participation, but company/group objectives can be more structured and goal accomplishment more easily attained.

7.5 GROUP DEVELOPMENT

7.5.1 How groups develop

The more individuals share in activities the more they interact. This leads to a discovery of shared perspectives and, frequently, shared goals. These are the seeds of group development.

Groups are not static entities; like individuals, they are dynamic and constantly changing. It is generally accepted that all groups develop over a four-stage period. Depending on members, task and resources, these stages vary in time-scale. However, not all groups pass peacefully through these four stages. Some groups disintegrate within the first or second stages, leaving tasks incomplete and people dissatisfied. If groups do happen to re-form they must return to stage 1 and restart the developmental process.

7.5.2 Stages of group development

Tuckman (1977) proposed a four-stage developmental model of how groups develop, one of several conceptual models existing in the area of group dynamics. Tuckman's model is fairly simplistic but reflects quite accurately how people assume a group identity and begin to operate as one.

Forming

Members meet, usually for the first time, and attempt to 'find' themselves a place in the group. It is a process of testing out the new environment.

(a) **Feeling:** Members experience anxiety and uncertainty in a new environment. They attempt to share feelings and risk disclosing personal information about themselves.

(b) **Task:** Members are unsure of how to go about their task, schedule or agenda. They find it difficult to evaluate one another's suggestions because they are unfamiliar with the task and each other.

(c) **Social:** Members search for a sense of personal identity in the new group and are inclined to rely on others for guidelines. Previous experience is discussed, but as yet sensitive issues are not broached.

(d) **Leader:** Authority is rarely questioned in this first phase. Members, unsure of themselves or their position, tend to accept and rely upon guidelines set out.

Storming

Members experience conflict in areas such as goals, norms, status. They clash over adoption of roles and much effort is made, through overt means, to clarify group task.

(a) **Feeling:** Members are vying for identity. They begin to question decisions, disagreeing with one another. For some, this stage is a challenge; for others, conflict inhibits.

(b) **Task:** Members openly express differences in opinions and task expectations.

(c) **Social:** Members feel more secure on a personal level and are more self-assertive in their statements and/or actions. The group has not yet 'gelled' and social relationships are still being tested. Norms and attitudes are in early stages.

(d) **Leader:** Members, becoming more assertive, feel free to question decisions and the leader is frequently challenged.

Norming

The group is beginning to experience an identity. Members become more accepting and group success, rather than individual success, provides a sense of unity and purpose.

(a) **Feeling:** Members have begun to accept each other; tolerance rather than conflict is the overriding feeling. Individuals feel much more secure within the group and start to experience satisfaction and cohesion.

(b) **Task:** There is more open and reasonable discussion in this stage, members recognising the need for co-operation and goodwill. Tasks and roles are assigned and accepted.

(c) **Social**: Members adapt to group structure. Harmonious interaction is at its peak with co-operation in every sphere.

(d) **Leader:** The leader is no longer challenged but accepted and trusted with the task of organising goal accomplishment. He is frequently helped by group members, who accept delegation of tasks for the good of the group.

Performing

The group's overriding aim is goal accomplishment.

(a) **Feeling:** Members experience unity of purpose, satisfaction and motivation.

(b) **Task:** Members unite in striving for task accomplishment. Frequently, creativity and evaluation are encouraged.

(c) **Social:** Members experience mutual support and encouragement. Bonds of friendship are formed. Attitudes gel and norms are accepted and obeyed.

(d) **Leader:** Similar to previous stage.

A group evolving through all four stages will develop into an effective and productive entity. Members will be co-operative and motivated, with tasks being accomplished on satisfying terms. As noted earlier, groups that fail to proceed at their own pace through these stages will not develop completely, nor will they be productive. Interestingly, once a specific task is completed, the group, on commencement of a new task, tends to retrace its steps through the same four stages. If group membership remains the same, stages 1 and 2 are passed through relatively quickly in order to re-experience the group cohesiveness and productivity exemplified in stages 3 and 4.

Although these four developmental stages occur in all groups, they are not as distinct as we have portrayed them. However, depending on the size and type of membership, it is often possible to identify a particular stage. This may be advantageous in a work situation where management, aware of group development dynamics, recognises, understands and responds to the group at its various levels of development.

Once a group has assumed an identity, having worked through the four stages, it becomes a very powerful factor.

7.6 GROUP POWER

7.6.1 Power

The power of a group lies in its ability to control its members and ensure they possess a shared frame of reference: that is, a shared view of a particular situation. This shared frame of reference not only aids goal accomplishment, but also ensures group survival. What happens when the group's power is questioned? Any deviations from the norms or any challenges are regarded as a threat. The group responds by closing ranks and imposing certain (usually agreed) sanctions such as fines or disbarment. Why do people 'obey' the group, or allow it so much power?

7.6.2 Reasons for conforming

People obey the group rather than risk exclusion. This conforming behaviour occurs for a number of reasons:

(a) **Fear of rejection:** If a person has worked hard to become a member of a group for whatever reason, they tend to accept roles/norms imposed by the group rather than suffer rejection.

(b) **Unanimity among members:** It is difficult to be a minority of one and to resist the pressures of a group of individuals. Psychological research indicates that when a group's unanimity is perforated, so also is its social power (Morris and Miller, 1975).

(c) **Perceived attractiveness:** If a group is perceived as attractive, desirable or possessing status, its rules will more than likely be accepted (Mullen, 1985).

(d) **Gains to be made:** If an individual perceives that gains are to be made by remaining in the group, a trade-off will ensue. He will accept group rules in return for gains.

(e) **Ambiguity of stimuli:** The greater the number of ways stimuli may be interpreted, the greater the likelihood of conformity by the group. In other words, where there is no one correct and obvious interpretation of a situation, individuals tend to reach group agreement. See Asch's (1956) experiment.

(f) **Degree of self-esteem/Personality variables:** It has been suggested (Hall and Lindzey, 1985) that there are connections between conforming behaviour and personality traits. Individuals requiring social approval tend to be more conforming in their behaviour.

7.6.3 Research in conformity

Conformity may be defined as 'a change in behaviour or belief . . . as a result of real or imagined group pressure' (Kiesler and Kiesler, 1969). It is the behavioural result of being affected by how others act as well as acting as others act.

The following two pieces of research highlight the conforming nature of individuals.

Asch's Line Experiment (1956)

Soloman Asch (a social psychologist) believed in the concept of conformity yet expressed reservations as to whether, when an unambiguous stimulus was presented, conforming behaviour would ensue.

His experiment consisted of seven subjects (one naïve and six confederates) and a series of trials depicting lines of various lengths. Confederates is the name used in psychology for individuals participating in an experiment instructed to act in a particular way by the experimenter. 'Naïve' refers to subjects unaware that the experimenter is manipulating his confederates. The task in this experiment was to match Line X with a line of similar length, i.e. A, B or C.

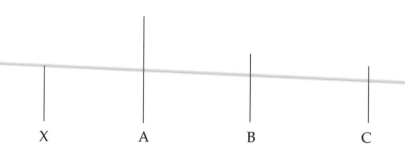

The six confederates or helpers were:

(a) unknown to the naïve subject

(b) instructed to make erroneous judgments on previously selected trials, i.e. they purposefully selected incorrect lines as previously agreed with Asch.

The naïve subject was placed second to last, therefore witnessing five volunteers' opinions, before being requested to give his own. In over one-third of the trials, the naïve subject agreed with the confederates in what were obviously incorrect selections. According to Asch, the naïve subject denied his own senses, preferring to agree with his cohorts and follow the norm set.

Milgram's Study of Obedience (1974)

Stanley Milgram's controversial experiment examined conformity to authority. Asch's (1956) and Sherif and Sherif's (1969) research highlighted covert group pressure to conform, i.e. where no clear pressure was put on individuals to conform. Milgram presented his experiment in an attempt to see how far people would respond to overt pressure in the guise of authority.

His experiment consisted of:

(a) confederates
(b) volunteers } matched one to one

(c) electric shock generator assessing intensity level, moderate through to fatal.

The experiment was presented to volunteers as the effects of punishment on learning abilities. A volunteer had to teach a confederate a series of word pairs. When errors were made in recall, the volunteer was instructed to administer an electric shock. The more errors made, the stronger the shock intensity. At this stage it is important to clarify several points:

(i) Milgram's aim was to see if ordinary individuals would obey the authority figure and knowingly administer various electric shocks to other humans.

(ii) Confederates were work colleagues of Milgram's and were NOT connected to any electrical apparatus, but instructed to scream when 'punished'.

(iii) Volunteers truly believed that they were administering waves of electrical currents to another individual (witnessed by the fact that volunteers sweated profusely, became agitated and visibly upset).

(iv) Pairs (one volunteer–one confederate) were seated one on each side of a screen; visual eye contact was blocked.

When Milgram described his intended experiments to a group of 110 psychiatrists, college students and middle-class adults, they responded thus:

(a) Self-estimates would not exceed 135 volts (between moderate and strong), i.e. if in a similar situation, they themselves would not administer very heavy electrical currents.

(b) Others might reach 'intense' level (300 volts), i.e. other people might go further (self-bias perception coming into play).

(c) No one expected the fatal dose to be administered.

(d) Psychiatrists suggested that the likelihood of (c) being reached would be one in 1,000, with that one individual being seriously mentally disturbed.

The results were highly unexpected, with 63 per cent of volunteers reaching 450 volts — fatal intensity — despite hearing supposedly agonised screams from behind the screen. Needless to say, Milgram's experiment was denounced as unethical; the imposition of mental/physical abuse in the name of psychological research is strictly forbidden. Nevertheless, it did point out that well over half his volunteers conformed to authority to the extent that they were willing to administer fatal electric shocks.

7.6.4 Hawthorne Studies

No work on groups would be complete without mention of the Hawthorne Studies. Carried out by Elton Mayo in the 1920s in Western Electric Plant, Chicago, USA, these studies were amongst the most extensive and influential in any area of social research.

Mayo, a member of the National Academy of Sciences, was invited to research the Theory of Effects of Altered Illumination on work procedures within the Hawthorne factory of the plant. Put simply, it was posited that the better the light the better the productivity. A two-group experimental design was carried out, with surprising results. Rather than only one group increasing its work rate (the group receiving brighter illumination), both groups' work increased. After repeated experiments with similar results, Mayo concluded that it was not the altered illumination which increased productivity but the fact that the workers concerned in the experiments were receiving extra attention from management. The so-named 'Hawthorne Effect' is that the extra attention given to individuals increases their sense of importance, which in turn enhances performance. We can see the Hawthorne Effect operate in everyday life; children as well as adults feel and perform better when acknowledged or when positive attention is paid to them.

Mayo stayed with Western Electric for a number of years to advance his research and became interested in group theory — how effective groups are within a working environment. His two famous pieces of research involved the Relay Room and Bank Wiring Room Experiments.

Relay Room

This involved six female workers, permitted to choose their own group of work colleagues, and observed over a period during which work rates, rest periods and finishing times were continuously altered. The aim was to establish under which conditions the women worked the hardest. In fact, the women's productivity rate increased regardless of whether conditions were altered positively or negatively. The following conclusions were drawn:

(a) Hawthorne Effect became operationalised — the women's sense of importance increased because they felt that they were helping the company to solve problems. Thus the conditions set out by management, i.e. work rates, were not influencing factors.

(b) Women felt a sense of belonging, stability and purpose in being part of their group.

These factors resulted in good relationships between women and supervisors, low absenteeism, higher motivation and record levels of production.

Bank Wiring Room

This involved male workers being observed by a neutral observer who concluded that:

(a) Natural leaders emerged within the group, and were not necessarily those appointed by management.

(b) Codes of conduct originated from, and were practised by, the group, e.g. norms, rules.

(c) The group instigated its own authority regulations without management having to supervise.

(d) Deviants from the group were punished by the group.

See Buchanan and Huczynski (1991) for detailed observations of the Hawthorne Studies. Ours is an overview of Mayo's work, which leads to the following conclusions:

(a) Informal groups will always form in work situations and possess a recognised structure.

(b) Work is essentially a group activity.

(c) Groups fulfil the needs for belonging, stability and security present in most people.

(d) Natural leaders emerge from groups.

(e) A worker is a person who tends to be conditioned by social demands of the work group.

(f) The informal work group is capable of exerting tremendous pressure on individuals to conform to group norms.

(g) Deviants are punished or isolated if the group is threatened.

Mayo's importance lies in the fact that he marked the beginning of the age of modern management theory. Mayo conceived workers as not purely motivated by money but also sensitive to personal attention in terms of management and co-workers. He felt that employees worked more productively and positively when a group atmosphere prevailed. Theorists such as Vroom and Adams endorsed Mayo's conclusions.

The presence of groups in our lives is pervasive. We do not and cannot exist in isolation. Any one of us is a member of at least three or four different categories of groups; we obey three or four different sets of norms and succumb to varying pressures to exhibit expected behaviour. Most of us do so unknowingly. An insight into group dynamics will, we hope, provide an insight into human behaviour — the goal of the behavioural scientist.

7.7 SUMMARY

1. A group is any number of people who interact, are psychologically aware of each other and share a group identity.
2. Individuals join groups for a variety of reasons, including security, affiliation, goals, activities and attraction.
3. Groups may be categorised in a number of ways, the most important being formal, informal and reference groups.
4. Group structure consists of cohesiveness, status, roles, norms, communication and size. The stable pattern of interaction between the members in relation to these characteristics comprises group structure.
5. There are four developmental stages: forming, storming, norming and performing.
6. Just as people have valid reasons for joining a group, they also have valid reasons for wishing to remain members.
7. Groups exert tremendous pressure on their members to conform. Experiments by Asch, Milgram and Sherif highlight such pressures.
8. The Hawthorne Studies are highly influential studies of group behaviour in a work situation. Their conclusions range from establishing the well-respected Hawthorne Effect to the premise that work is a group activity.

7.8 EXAM QUESTIONS

1. Define a group. Discuss why people join and wish to remain members of groups.
2. Assess the extent to which group membership influences people's beliefs, attitudes and behaviour. (MII, 1989)
3. Discuss the part played by norms in group structure.
4. Describe the four stages of group development and how a knowledge of them might aid an organisational merger.
5. How do the structures within a group help explain the behaviour of group members? (MII, 1992)

8   8

Organisations and Organisational Behaviour

8.1   INTRODUCTION

8.2   ORGANISATIONAL EXPERIENCE
         8.2.1 What is an organisation?
         8.2.2 Organisational concepts
         8.2.3 Theoretical approaches to organisations
         8.2.4 Organisational technology
         8.2.5 Organisational recruitment

8.3   INTERACTION BETWEEN HUMAN AND
         ORGANISATIONAL BEHAVIOUR
         8.3.1 Organisational communication
         8.3.2 Organisational change
         8.3.3 Psychological contract

8.4   SUMMARY

8.5   EXAM QUESTIONS

Learning Objectives

After studying this chapter you should be able to:

— *Define the terms 'organisation' and 'organisational behaviour'*
— *Recognise three theoretical organisational perspectives*
— *Understand the importance of an organisational communication system and its concomitant problems*
— *Discuss the implications of technology within an organisation*
— *Evaluate the problems and solutions encountered when organisational change is introduced*
— *Understand two main approaches to staff recruitment along with the concept of 'psychological contract'.*

8.1 INTRODUCTION

Up to this point we have examined the behaviour of individuals within a somewhat general environment. Now we examine the interrelationships and dynamics of humans within the business world, within corporate entities, within organisations. As we shall see, organisations have their own characteristics; how these develop and interact with the workforce is the subject of much study and discussion. In order to understand employee behaviour we must understand organisations, for one influences the other.

In this chapter we examine the make-up of organisations and their ability to exist in an often-changing environment. Knowledge gained from previous chapters, in such areas as perception, learning and motivation, enhances our awareness of potential interaction between worker and organisation.

This interaction is commonly referred to as organisational behaviour. As we know, rarely, if ever, does anything occur in isolation. It is the same within organisations. We have to view them, their workforce and their environment as one. In order to do this we must take a Gestalt approach: i.e. realise that the whole is greater than the sum of its parts, the parts being:

(a) human experience

(b) organisational experience

(c) interaction or interface between human and organisation.

This three-tier approach is important. We can focus on any of these parts individually, but for a comprehensive understanding of organisations and organisational behaviour, we must recognise the interrelatedness of all three.

Human experience

We understand from previous chapters how individuals, or in this case employees:

(a) acquire attitudes

(b) possess perceptions

(c) learn skills

(d) become motivated,

all of which contribute to a person's unique perspective on his working environment and work ethos. Essentially the 'human experience' variable refers to personal characteristics and experiences brought to the workplace by employees.

Organisational experience

This encompasses:

(a) various organisational concepts

(b) theoretical approaches to organisations

(c) technology

(d) recruitment procedures.

These factors refer, generally, to the structure, development and operation of the company.

Interaction between human and organisation

The final tier basically refers to relationships and interactions between workers and management, encompassing such factors as:

(a) organisational communication

(b) organisational change

(c) psychological contract.

8.2 ORGANISATIONAL EXPERIENCE

8.2.1 What is an organisation?

An organisation is a group of people working together to attain common goals. A more complex definition offers 'a purposeful social unit of people carrying out differentiated tasks/activities which are co-ordinated by one or more managers to contribute to the organisation's goals' (Moorhead and Griffin, 1992).

Regardless of which definition is used, the concept of 'co-ordination' is implicit. That is, to be organised is to be co-ordinated. Co-ordination is accomplished only by allowing our behaviour to be directed by others. Recognition of this fact leads individuals voluntarily to relinquish some of their flexibility or freedom. The term 'organisation', therefore, implies a trade-off between personal independence and organisational goal achievement. How this trade-off is accomplished is the core of organisational behaviour and the focus of our chapter. We must first, however, understand on a broader scale the functioning of an organisation.

8.2.2 Organisational concepts

An organisation is frequently described as a large group. Our knowledge of group concepts teaches us that groups have structure, development and characteristics; a corollary is that organisations possess similar attributes. Organisations are often referred to as having profiles, similar to individuals: hard-working, forward-looking, etc. In order to familiarise the reader with organisational concepts, we have selected several of the most widely used, or generic, terms employed in discussing organisational matters.

Organisational development: the process of planned changes and improvements through application of behavioural science knowledge, i.e. learning, motivation, attitudes.

Organisational structure: system of task reporting and authority relationships existing within an organisation, i.e. hierarchy of authority.

Organisational culture: beliefs and attitudes, i.e. set of values that help employees to learn what is acceptable or unacceptable behaviour.

Organisational characteristics: overall structure, culture, technology and design of the organisation.

Organisational environment: financial resources, economy, legislative aspects outside organisational boundaries, e.g. 'green' legislation, EC policies.

Organisational process: processes of decision-making, creativity, communication and performance appraisal, e.g. delegation/shared responsibility, promotional prospects.

Organisations, regardless of size, structure or purpose, tend to share certain characteristics that facilitate smooth co-ordination and operation:

a) division of labour

b) common goals

c) hierarchy of authority.

Division of labour refers to sectionalisation or departmentalisation. Whether it is applied in the case of photocopying or mail delivery (as in larger companies) or in allocating to one person the responsibility for buying stamps (as in a smaller company), the overall effect is similar. Workers learn expected behaviour, time is saved and expertise/knowledge is usually gained.

Common goals refers to the organisation as a whole (management and staff) possessing a shared frame of reference, a common viewpoint. The sharing of common goals provides unity of purpose, aids evaluation of functioning and promotes an individual's sense of purpose and belonging, e.g. achieving a new work contract over foreign competitors.

Hierarchy of authority refers to the necessity of having a recognised authority system (workers know who they have to report to), which promotes the functioning of the organisation, ensures performance and is a means of allocating status.

8.2.3 Theoretical approaches to organisations

Organisational design co-ordinates the efforts of people and departments. Designs must maximise efficiency, co-ordination and accomplishment. Three perspectives or approaches have influenced organisational design: namely the Classical approach, Systems approach and Human Relations approach. Each highlights a particular organisational orientation ranging from the highly structured universal approach to the more relaxed social approach.

Classical approach

Emerging from the Scientific Management ethos, Classical organisation theorists, borrowing terms such as efficiency and discipline, focused on how organisations could be structured most effectively. Whilst Scientific Management centred on scientifically controlled person/job interaction, Classical theorists centred on the concepts of logic, rationality and efficiency of the organisation itself. They looked at how workers and management could be effectively organised into an overall structure. Key Classical theorists included Henri Fayol and Max Weber.

Weber's Bureaucracy

At the beginning of this century, Weber, a German lawyer, introduced the word 'Bureaucracy' into organisational language, with stability, control and predictability as the goals of any organisation. Bureaucracy offered a logical, rational and efficient *modus operandi*. Weber proffered that an administration characterised by a hierarchy of authority, rules and regulations could and would work for all organisations regardless of size. That is, he proposed a more or less universal structure based on the assumption of efficiency.

Weber's Bureaucracy has seven basic elements devised to maximise efficiency and order amongst the workforce and job design. The following table encapsulates these elements:

Elements	Comments
1. Rules and procedures	A consistent set of rules and procedures to ensure uniform performance
2. Distinct division of labour	Each position to be filled by an expert

3. Hierarchy of authority	Clearly established chain of command
4. Technical competence	Merit and competence should be basis of promotion and recruitment
5. Segregation of ownership	Professional managers, rather than owners, should run the organisation
6. Rights and properties of the position	Should be associated with the organisation, not the person who holds the office
7. Documentation	Record of all administrative decisions, rules, etc. should be maintained

Today, unfortunately, Bureaucracy is a term which tends to possess negative connotations; words such as inflexibility and red tape are often used synonymously. Indeed, criticism of Weber's model has been widespread, including accusations of:

(a) **rigidity**, both in structure and authority

(b) **impersonality**, which may lead to communication problems between employee and employer

(c) **ignorance of the human element:** It does not recognise the individuality of motivation, perceptions, or the principles of group behaviour

(d) **mechanical approach:** Workers must fit into the organisation, regardless of abilities or motivations.

Nevertheless, Classical theory remains very much the cornerstone of business organisations today. The goals of organisational order, efficiency and predictability are considered worthwhile against the backdrop of somewhat rigid authoritarian rule. Out of this approach — or perhaps because of it — a new perspective emerged, eschewing rigidity in favour of flexibility, and recognising the existence of a wider organisational picture: the Systems perspective.

Systems approach

Systems theory views organisations as a set of interrelated elements functioning as a whole. Because of this, it is often referred to as the socio-technical system. This approach offers delegation, job enrichment and a more flexible approach to organisational design than Weber's Bureaucratic structure. It is an approach conscious of the 'fit' between an organisation and its environment; i.e. it looks at the Gestalt of the organisation. Implicit in this theory is the concept of open and closed organisational designs: open referring to those organisations receptive to and sharing with their environment; closed referring to those organisations tending to operate in isolation, disregarding the economic climate. This may appear contradictory in relation to Systems theory premise; nevertheless it differs in degree rather than in design.

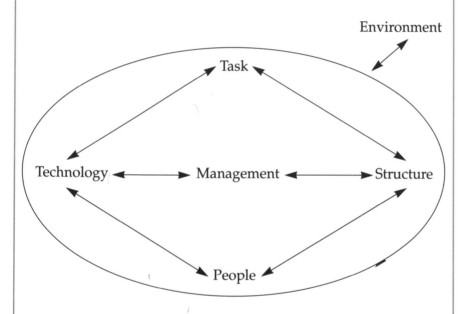

An extension of the Systems design is referred to as the Contingency approach. In many organisations, situations and outcomes are contingent upon one another. The relationship between any two variables is likely to be influenced by other existing variables. For example, the standards of worker behaviours (outputs) will be affected by the type of feedback received from society (environment) at large. If legislation forbids the pollution of air, the organisation will have to alter its inputs/transformation sections to comply. All sectors of the organisation are contingent or dependent on each other. The whole picture is a series of interacting systems.

Frequently, the Systems theory is presented as the Socio-Technical Systems theory wherein individual social and technical elements replace the inputs variable (as in the diagram below). Rather than clubbing human and material elements together, the Socio-Technical model distinguishes between them.

In effect, four systems exist:

(a) Internal social system

(b) Internal technical system

(c) Internal overall system with the different variables co-ordinating

(d) The organisation as an entity co-operating with the environment, itself a system.

It is important to be aware that all four systems should be balanced, i.e. management cannot afford to sacrifice, say, the social for the technical subsystem. Researchers in the Tavistock Institute in the United Kingdom (Trist and Banforth, 1951) suggested that this had actually happened in the British coal-mining industry when management tried to increase productivity by reorganising work schedules and introducing new mining techniques. They failed to recognise the adverse effects this would have on the existing social system, such as breaking up long-standing work groups and moving colleagues to other areas. In an effort to overcome the problems that had arisen, the Tavistock researchers proposed the introduction of autonomous work groups. Although co-ordinated by management, these worker groups were responsible for job assignments, training, inspection, rewards and punishment within their specific areas.

The Socio-Technical system saw management role not as authoritarian but as monitoring and co-ordinating both the environment and the organisation so that the two were compatible.

One of the main differences between Classical and Systems theories is that while the former espouses a fairly rigid hierarchy, the latter posits a more flexible arrangement emphasising management co-ordination.

Human Relations approach

The third approach differs from the previous two in that it focuses exclusively on the human factor, adopting basic premises such as an individual's needs for recognition, belonging and potential for self-fulfilment. Attention shifts away from the study of man/job efficiency towards a fuller understanding of the nature of interpersonal and group relations within the organisation. Organisational orientation is characterised by a strong social emphasis.

The Human Relations perspective admits to sharing the basic goal of management: to secure employee compliance with managerial authority. This is occasioned by emphasising and satisfying the needs of employees, primarily through interpersonal strategies, rather than changing the nature of the job. Perhaps the most famous investigation of Human Relations approach at work is the Hawthorne Studies (details of which are given in Chapter 7).

Contemporary thinking in this sphere suggests that the Human Relations perspective is somewhat idealistic in that recognition of individual workers' needs and social wants could tie up both time and resources. For example, one individual may value having his security needs met whilst another may value only financial gains — such a differentiation would utilise valuable management time. It must be recognised that many other factors are also capable of influencing organisational behaviour, e.g. supervisory styles and environmental demands.

The following table summarises the three approaches from a managerial viewpoint:

Classical	Systems	Human Relations
Close supervision and control	Delegates and co-ordinates	Makes workers feel useful and important
Establishes work procedures and policies	Co-ordinates social and technical systems into integrated whole	Allows workers to exercise self-direction and self-control
Rigid hierarchy	Democratic	Attends to social factors

Although the three perspectives differ, each possesses positive and negative points. For example, although the Classical approach is fairly rigid, the workforce is afforded the security of knowing exactly what job it has to do and how the authority hierarchy works. The Systems approach may encourage overdue familiarity but democratic co-ordination provides the foundation-stone for the organisation. The Human Relations stance promotes interpersonal relationships and goodwill, thus relying on a knock-on effect to increase productivity, rather than any stringent rules or regulations.

All three perspectives share a similar aim — to enhance worker–organisation efficiency. Our next section examines a factor which complements this efficiency, organisational technology.

8.2.4 Organisational technology

In theory, technology refers to any mechanical/intellectual process by which inputs are transformed into outputs (Moorhead and Griffen, 1992). Organisational technology refers to a successful match between an organisation's structure and its technology: in other words, its effectiveness in 'integrating technology structure, personal characteristics and social factors into a congruent goal-orientated entity' (Steers, 1993).

Technology has a profound impact on an organisation, particularly from a survival viewpoint. It affects the organisation across the board, from personnel to productivity. When deciding upon the introduction of new technology, management will frequently engage in the following simplified model of management decision-making:

WHAT	What are the capabilities of technology?
WHY	What are the organisation's objectives in introducing such technology? Will it aid management goals?
HOW	How do we successfully implement technical changes within the organisation structure?
CONSEQUENCES	Possible increase/decrease in employment Improved skills/knowledge base Improved quality of working life Change in role of management Change in levels of productivity/profit.

Management's task is to consider the merits of new technology and how best to implement it within the overall organisational structure. From a workforce viewpoint, however, this poses a serious question: does it mean an increase in skills and knowledge or does it really mean loss of job security? Fears in the latter case have, in the past, proved well founded. The introduction of new technology is fraught with problems. Will workers resent the change and refuse to co-operate? Will the technology be too costly and too advanced? Will it necessitate employing experts? In an effort to alleviate such problems, management introduces 'Compensatory Mechanisms', processes that attempt to overcome the negative impact of technical change. These include:

(a) increasing employee awareness of why changes have been implemented, e.g. to maintain market position

(b) providing training courses for workers to use the new technology

(c) highlighting the fact that quite often the introduction of new technology enables the organisation to produce new products or services at a lower, more stable cost. This in turn increases consumer demand, with the corollary of increased worker demand.

The implementation of organisational change, whether technological or structural, is potentially troublesome. See 8.3.2, where the issue has been dealt with in greater detail.

8.2.5 Organisational recruitment

Recruiting staff is now considered a highly important psychological task with far-reaching implications in areas such as finances, performance levels, staff morale and interpersonal relationships. It is vital that new employees integrate well, fit in with co-workers, and feel in general that they belong to the organisation. This matching process incorporates two common approaches to employee recruitment: Selection approach and Classification approach.

Selection approach

This is the more traditional model. The organisation attempts to match an individual with the position; the person must fit the needs of the organisation. Application forms, interviews, personality and aptitude tests are all employed to find the 'right' employee and, as can be imagined, the process is both time-consuming and expensive. This approach employs scientific techniques (measurement) and has two aspects:

(a) defining the physical, academic and psychological requirements of the job by drawing up a job description, e.g. the required levels of performance, psychological demands and levels of responsibility. Once important job attributes have been identified, e.g. initiative and flexibility, they are tested against performance criteria (match the doing of the job). These are then defined as the key attributes prospective candidates should possess.

(b) selecting individual to match. Companies often prefer to adopt a fairly structured interview procedure or framework involving an interview board, whose task is to assess all aspects of the interviewee. Questions asked are frequently decided beforehand, with each board member taking responsibility for a certain area, e.g. expertise, personal history. Whatever the interview structure, the interviewee will be invited to answer questions that elicit information about:

(i) intelligence/common sense/initiative

(ii) disposition, e.g. attitudes to responsibility

(iii) special attributes, e.g. languages, computer skills

(iv) circumstances, e.g. marital status, children, interests.

Although this approach is the most widely used recruitment method, it offers very little in the way of clear-cut or standardised performance levels from either employer or employee perspectives. For example, we have learned that interviewers are prone to perceptual errors (stereotyping, halo effect), while employees will often attempt to say or do what they think is expected of them in order to enhance their appeal.

Classification approach

This approach focuses on fitting the job to the person. One recruits an individual with a proven track record, designing a job around him in order to utilise his best attributes. Employers concentrate on making the job attractive to the prospective employee by attending to such matters as:

(a) beneficial physical environment, e.g. own office, company car, pension and health contributions

(b) aids to production capabilities, e.g. selection of latest technology, team back-up, financial allocations — all to ease and enhance performance

(c) social interaction, e.g. the company doing its utmost to ensure that this individual is made to feel welcome and accepted.

The emphasis of this approach is on meeting the employee's expectations and demands.

Both approaches have the same goal, to ensure that the 'fit' between individual and organisation is mutually rewarding. Today, all organisations face the challenge of recruiting from and managing an increasingly diverse workforce (dual-career families, job-sharing applicants).

8.3 INTERACTION BETWEEN HUMAN AND ORGANISATIONAL BEHAVIOUR

8.3.1 Organisational communication

We all know the importance of communication. If we cannot communicate effectively, we are misunderstood, misread and eventually isolated. So what is communication? It is 'the process by which two or more parties exchange information and share meaning' (O'Reilly and Pondy, 1979). Within organisational behaviour it refers not only to the ability to communicate with superiors, subordinates and colleagues, but also the ability to recognise potential problems or barriers. The communication process in fact forms the basis of an organisation, facilitating:

(a) interpersonal relationships

(b) information-sharing/decision-making/feedback

(c) co-ordination of activities/motivation

(d) goal direction.

The following diagram illustrates the basic model of communication that is applicable not only to interpersonal relationships but also to organisational communication.

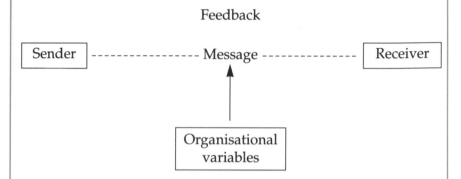

Like interpersonal relationships, an organisation faces problems if its communication system breaks down or is distorted. For the sake of brevity we summarise problems associated with each stage of our communication model.

Sender variable

(a) **Filtering/Withholding:** When sending a message, the sender may choose to filter or withhold parts. In other words, only certain sections of the message may be sent in the mistaken belief that such information is released on a need-to-know basis. This course of action can have two serious consequences:

(i) **erroneous interpretation** because information scarcity may cause mistakes to be made

(ii) **incomplete messages** rendered meaningless to everyone except the sender.

(b) **Encoding:** the sending of messages in an understandable form. There are several points to be aware of:

(i) **lack of common experience:** Frequently senders fail to realise that their experience is not shared by others. For example, it is no use issuing instructions on how to correct computer errors if the receiver of the message has no experience in computers.

(ii) **semantics:** word meanings and the difference in possible interpretations. For example, management may issue a work directive announcing how bad business is, employees may 'read' this as redundancies being in the pipeline.

(iii) **jargon:** the specialised or technical language used by various professions or groups of people, such as accountants, engineers. It has both a positive and a negative aspect from the communication point of view. The former consists of increasing efficiency and time savings — if the jargon is understood by all concerned, long-winded discussions or explanations are redundant. The disadvantage of using jargon is that it reinforces the in-group/ out-group situation — if you are not part of the in-group, jargon serves only to increase alienation.

Receiver variable

(a) **Selective attention:** where the receiver attends to only part of the message. In other words, he selects the section which he thinks applies to him (usually from a cue word), and heeds only that.

(b) **Value judgments:** where the receiver acknowledges the message to the degree to which it either reinforces or challenges his beliefs. In other words, if the message agrees with the receiver's feelings/ thoughts about the topic, the value judgment will be positive. Take an annual salary review situation: if employees are informed that reviews will be low due to a turn-down in production/profit levels, they proceed to make value judgments in accordance with their own perception of the situation. Depending on whether perceptions agree or disagree, the statement or message will be either accepted or rejected.

(c) **Credibility:** if the sender of the message is regarded in a positive light, i.e. perceived as an expert or at least seen to know what he is talking about. Credibility fails when workforces disregard or ridicule the sender and consequently ignore the message itself.

(d) **Overload:** simply where too much information, be it instructions or memoranda, is piled onto the receiver, often resulting in non-action.

Feedback variable

The biggest communication failure in this area is the omission of feedback to the sender. Feedback is of utmost importance in the communication chain because it allows for clarification, verification, encouragement and motivation. It is an indication of message receipt and the degree to which it has been understood. Feedback is quite often received non-verbally, i.e. through facial expressions and body language.

Organisational variables

(a) **Noise:** any disturbance within the communication network that interferes with or distorts communication, e.g. rumours, gossip, misinterpretations.

(b) **Status difference:** If the hierarchy or authority chain is somewhat rigid, communication tends to be one-way, top to bottom. True communication is a two-way relationship so organisations must ensure that workers have the necessary feedback or communication forum.

(c) **Time pressures/Overload:** similar to receiver overload. If an organisation does not allow sufficient time/space for a workforce to cope with information demands, the communication chain will become logged.

(d) **Communication structure:** Organisations must ensure that their communication structure is two-way, communication occurring not only top/down but vice versa. The workforce must perceive itself as having (and in fact must have) a forum, be it monthly meetings or more informal contact, which provides an opportunity to open communication with management.

Interestingly, according to Ralph Nicholas, as far back as 1962 (Steers, 1991) the percentage of information filtered out during downward communications amounts to approximately 80 per cent.

	%
Top management's understanding of message	100
Vice-president's understanding of message	63
General manager's understanding of message	56
Plant manager's understanding of message	40
Supervisor's understanding of message	30
Worker and final message	20

When upward communication does occur, it tends to be influenced by:

(i) what the worker thinks his superior wants to know

(ii) highlighting or exaggeration of positive aspects

(iii) omission or downplay of negative aspects.

The basic premise of organisational communication is to provide the right information to the right person at the right time and in the right place. This sounds simple enough, but we have seen the problems that can arise. So how does an organisation avoid them? Two general routes suggest themselves:

(i) **Reduce noise:** 'Noise' or distortion blocks and misinterprets communication through what is generally known as the office grapevine. To overcome this, management should effectively use and monitor the grapevine to know exactly what is being said and so introduce an element of control.

(ii) **Foster informal communication:** Organisations tend to have fairly structured communication patterns, but it is important to allow for flexibility. Communication must be permitted to take place not only up/down and vice versa but also horizontally. Top/down communication lends itself to issuing goals, strategies, procedures whilst upward communication lends itself to communication of problems, grievances and performance reports. Horizontal communication, on the other hand, allows for co-ordination between management and staff in so far as it permits intra-departmental and inter-departmental communication and problem-solving.

The communication pattern adopted by any organisation depends on many factors, including:

(a) authority structure — autocratic or democratic

(b) task design — what type of business is involved

(c) size of organisation — number of employees.

Four well-known communication patterns exist for organisational networks:

(i) **Wheel network:** Communication flows between the person at the end of each spoke and the person in the centre. Communication is restricted and information tends to be centralised.

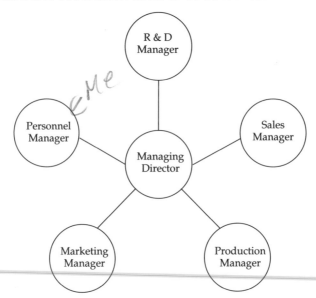

(ii) **Chain network:** Members communicate with those above and below but not with individuals at each end.

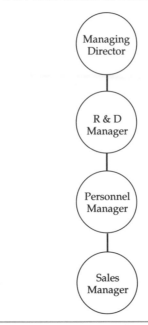

(iii) **Circle network:** Each member communicates with individuals on both sides but with no one else.

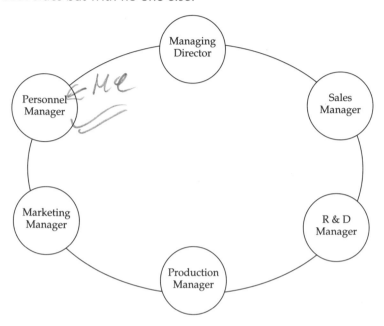

(iv) **All-channel network:** All members communicate with each other.

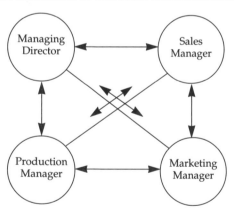

Communication is a complex and dynamic process, vital not only to effective organisational co-ordination, but also to organisational achievement. It is a potentially problematic area so management must ensure that lines of communication are kept open and unhindered at all times.

8.3.2 Organisational change

We live in a constantly changing and dynamic environment. Not only are our thoughts, ideas and attitudes constantly being challenged, but so also is our working environment. Organisations too face the challenge of the environment. For example, forces of change impinging upon an organisation include:

(a) Government/Legislation/Economy

(b) Financial/Human resources

(c) Competitors/Markets.

Part of management's role is to recognise when some form of change is required. Triggers for organisational change tend to fall into two categories: external and internal.

External triggers

(a) **Technological:** Artificial intelligence has meant that information is processed and disseminated more quickly. Satellite, portable and conference phones all enhance today's communication system; an organisation must keep abreast of improvements.

(b) **Governmental:** New consumer laws, legislation, ecological awareness campaigns and growing European markets precipitate continuous policy changes.

(c) **Economy and markets:** The sharing and opening up of European communities heightens awareness of international market trends. For example, the growing strength of large conglomerates buying out their smaller competitors emphasises the need for market vigilance.

(d) **Research availability:** This refers to raw material costs/availability. An unexpected increase or unavailability in a major input (such as oil) could necessitate change.

Internal triggers

(a) **Organisational structure:** An organisation may have to be restructured, e.g. policy-making and centralisation procedures may have to be changed.

(b) **Organisational goals:** A change in goals may have to occur, e.g. rather than striving to be a brand leader, a company may have to diversify.

(c) **Technological:** Changes may result in replacement of part of the workforce by computers, leading to an emphasis of recruitment in computer-literate workforce.

Change is rarely welcomed within an organisation yet it must occur in order for the company to survive. Resistance, or indeed potential resistance, to change must be recognised and dealt with effectively. Change not only affects organisational structure but has repercussions for the workforce on a personal level. For example:

(a) **Security:** Change alters the security of employment and the day-to-day 'habits' of the workforce, often through alteration in tasks and/or reporting relationships.

(b) **Fear of the unknown:** When change occurs people fear the worst. Questions such as 'How will I cope?' and 'What will the new boss be like?' contribute to employee anxiety and stress and tend to result in poor performance levels.

(c) **Economic factors:** Change often has financial implications for the workforce; salaries and bonus schemes may be altered.

(d) **Social factors:** Change often breaks up the social network and group dynamics that have developed within the workforce. We are aware from our knowledge of groups (Chapter 7) how important this aspect of work is for the employee.

If change is accompanied by so much resistance, how is it possible to implement change procedures? Moorhead and Griffin (1992) suggest several strategies that management may adopt to decrease employee negativity.

(a) **Education and communication:** This centres on open communication and the supplying of information and knowledge to the workforce. Individuals, once armed with knowledge, automatically become less fearful and resistant. It is important that information-giving takes place in advance of the changes and not in retrospect.

(b) **Participation and involvement:** By involving the relevant employees in designing and planning change, resistance may be reduced. Employees may feel they have some control over the procedure.

(c) **Facilitation and support:** This refers to the emotional support and commitment given by management to employees who may experience change-related anxiety/stress in their work areas.

(d) **Negotiation and agreement:** Mutual goal-settling sessions are important in allaying fears and can only enhance change implementation.

(e) **Coercion:** Not widely recommended, this meets resistance with threatened pay reductions, job losses, or demotions. Such a path may be successful short-term but has obvious long-term negative consequences.

Change is a necessary part of life. Management must accurately assess the nature of, and the need for, change. It is also necessary for management to realise that the manner in which change is implemented is at least as important for success as the change itself.

8.3.3 Psychological contract

This is an implicit contract between employee and employer, acknowledging the employment relationship as an exchange process, involving mutual expectations and performance levels. Frequently this type of contract is non-verbalised, which may cause problems in that no shared frame of reference exists as to appropriate and acceptable behaviours. See 8.3.1 on the importance of open communication within organisational life.

The parties' expectations within the employment relationship may be summarised as follows:

Expectations

Employer	*Employee*
1. recognition of individual rights in exchange for compliance	1. rewards for outputs (salary, security)
2. legitimate work demands (outputs, performance)	2. treated with dignity and respect
3. acceptance of company objectives by employee	3. acceptance of organisational authority

Organisational behaviour encompasses a broad area of study. We have addressed the fundamentals of the subject, providing a framework for understanding how organisations operate in today's changing and challenging environment.

8.4 SUMMARY

1. An organisation is a group of people working towards the same goals. Organisational behaviour comprises the human experience, the organisation experience and the interaction between the two.
2. Three organisational perspectives exist: Classical (rigid and somewhat authoritarian), Systems (co-ordination between social, technical and environmental aspects) and Human Relations (social dynamic) approaches.
3. Technology is vital for organisational survival. Introduction causes problems which must be addressed by management.
4. The Selection and Classification approaches to staff recruitment match, respectively, person to job and job to person.
5. Communication is a vital part of organisational life. Management must be aware of potential problems and attempt solutions.
6. The concept of change can be threatening to an organisational workforce, which may offer various avenues of resistance. Management must be prepared to spend time and effort allaying fears.
7. The implicit contract between employer and employee, called the psychological contract, views employment as an exchange process.

8.5 EXAM QUESTIONS

1. What is an organisation? Explain what is meant by 'organisational behaviour'.
2. Compare and contrast the management roles of each of the three organisational perspectives.
3. Consider the problems encountered by management when introducing change into an organisation.
4. Explain the communication process.
5. What is the 'psychological contract'?

9   9

Culture and Society

9.1   INTRODUCTION

9.2   CULTURE
9.2.1 Expressions of culture
9.2.2 Subcultures
9.2.3 Characteristics of culture
9.2.4 Components of culture

9.3   SOCIETY
9.3.1 Socialisation
9.3.2 Agencies of socialisation
9.3.3 Mechanisms of socialisation
9.3.4 Norms
9.3.5 Roles
9.3.6 Social class
9.3.7 Status

9.4   SUMMARY

9.5   EXAM QUESTIONS

Learning Objectives

After studying this chapter you should be able to:

— *Understand the importance of culture and society in relation to individual behaviour*
— *Define and describe the characteristics and components of culture*
— *Describe and evaluate the socialisation process*
— *Evaluate the mechanisms of society in shaping human behaviour*
— *Discuss the concept of social class and its place within society.*

9.1 INTRODUCTION

In the preceding chapters we have studied human behaviour on an individual level (attitudes, motivation and perception) and at group level (groups and organisations). In order to understand human behaviour more fully, we must place our observations within a wider context, and examine the influence on behaviour of cultural and societal rules. This chapter presents an 'overview' or 'Gestalt' of the human condition, contributing to the picture we have drawn of factors influencing human behaviour.

Henry James, the nineteenth-century psychologist, once suggested that the world of the new-born infant could be likened to a 'booming, buzzing confusion', in that all sights and sounds were completely novel. In growing up, an infant must learn to translate this booming buzzing confusion into a lifestyle within his own culture. The diagram below represents the interactiveness of variables that play a part in this learning process:

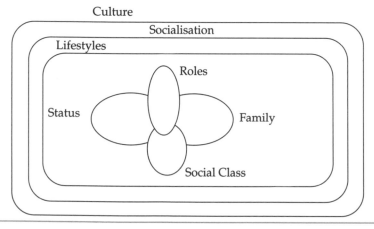

For simplicity, the chapter is divided into two parts. The first examines culture — how it is absorbed, passed down from generation to generation and affects our collective behaviours. The second part identifies society and its powerful influences through mechanisms such as norms, roles and lifestyles. Together, culture and society more or less determine our behaviours.

9.2 CULTURE

Culture is difficult to define. Kluckhohn (1951) notes that it is 'the distinctive way of life of a group of people, their complete design for living'. In other words, culture is shared by a group of people, is learned, distinctive and involves a lifestyle. Sociologists often refer to culture as the totality of those man-made attitudes, values, beliefs and mechanisms (mental and physical) that represent a life pattern of a particular group or society.

9.2.1 Expressions of culture

Cultures are frequently differentiated by means of national boundaries. However, in today's ever-changing world, natural boundaries are fast disappearing, and rather than allow cultures or lifestyles to disappear, people are clinging more strongly to the roots of their cultural identity. It has become common practice for emigrants to bring particular aspects of their culture to their adopted homelands. We see this happening, for example, within Asian communities in Britain, where arranged marriages are still very much in evidence. This transportation of culture provides for new immigrants a sense of continuity and security in what is often a vastly different and hostile land.

9.2.2 Subcultures

Subcultures are evident world-wide. Once subsumed within the prevalent culture, they are now becoming increasingly noticeable with people retaining much of their original lifestyles and habits. We have deliberately highlighted the nationalistic element of subcultures as it tends to be the most easily recognised, but subcultures also exist in terms of

(a) religion (Hindus, Muslims)

(b) age (young, elderly)

(c) sexual orientation (heterosexual, homosexual).

People belonging to a subculture, whatever its make-up, feel a sense of identity and belonging.

The gelling or cohabiting of nationalistic subcultures is seldom achieved without problems, hence the increase of racism. We see evidence of this in Germany, for example, where Turkish immigrants are continuously harassed by extreme right-wing nationalistic forces. In Britain Pakistanis are targeted by the National Front, and on our own island racism manifests itself in nationalist and loyalist murders.

9.2.3 Characteristics of culture

All cultures possess characteristics or distinctive features:

(a) **Culture is learned:** We absorb aspects of culture. For example, the effect of Catholicism is deeply rooted within the Irish psyche, as are the notions of superstition and fatalism. Emigrants, in a desire to be at one with their adoptive homelands, often willingly adopt and learn indigenous ideologies and values. This was certainly the case at the beginning of the century when thousands flocked to New York with the sole aim of becoming 'American'.

(b) **Culture serves the needs of society:** Culture provides a sense of continuity and structure for societies. Fulfilling much the same role as groups do for people, culture meets the needs of identity, security and affiliation. We see many Irish people using the Irish spelling of their names, speaking the Irish language at home and placing their children in Irish-speaking schools.

(c) **Culture is cumulative and adaptive:** Culture is an accumulation of customs, rituals, beliefs and values with each new era adding to this cultural storehouse. It is also adaptive, responding — albeit slowly — to shifts of belief and opinion within society. We can see the difference between today's Ireland and Éamon de Valera's ideal Ireland of the 1930s.

9.2.4 Components of culture

The components of culture provide mechanisms through which society's well-being and continuance are ensured. The expression of these components reflects the state of society. For example:

(a) **Institutions**
Institutions provide an organised system of behavioural rules or norms for a society, such as:

(i) **conventions:** appropriate patterns of behaviour in any given situation. They are society's unwritten rules for acceptance and appropriate behaviour: for example, all forms of social etiquette. The penalties for transgression of conventions are slight and frequently waived.

(ii) **mores:** strong moral sanctions. They are the most important social norms of behaviour, encompassing such areas as fidelity in marriage, the forbidding of incest and murder, and the recognition of immoral acts. Mores tend to be codified in law (as with forbidding murder/incest).

(iii) **laws:** formal recognitions of appropriate/inappropriate behaviours. They reflect society's views at any particular time and exist to ensure the continuance and well-being of society. It is important to realise that laws do change, usually reflecting a change in cultural ideas and mores. For example, it is no longer unlawful for a man to marry his dead wife's sister.

(b) **Ideas**
Culture, because it is adaptive, recognises the necessity of adopting an era's values, beliefs and attitudes. Values within a society provide standards of comparison for its people. For example, Irish culture stresses the value of family life. Beliefs refer to states of knowledge. The beliefs of the Irish nation are very much intertwined with Catholicism and nationalism. Attitudes are feelings. Today's Irish people's feelings are less accepting of Catholic Church influence.

(c) **Materials**
Materials may be described as the physical expressions of the human state. They form the link between a culture's knowledge base and its artefacts or tools, such as arts, literature and technology. Culture is

frequently expressed through the arts. Every culture has its own songs and poetry providing people with a sense of the past. Ireland has its traditional music and England its folk-songs.

Culture reflects, at any particular time, the state of society.

9.3 SOCIETY

In order to survive, individuals must learn to live in harmony, and to do this they must recognise, understand and adopt acceptable behavioural patterns. This process is known as socialisation.

9.3.1 Socialisation

Socialisation may be defined as the process of learning to live in a society by adopting socially acceptable behaviour. It is 'the means by which society prepares the individual for the role/s he is expected to play, whether personal, work or social'. The culture in which an individual lives determines how this socialisation process develops.

Basically socialisation has two main functions:

(a) It prepares an individual for his place in society, from teaching a child necessary life skills to learning what is acceptable and appropriate behaviour.

(b) It ensures continuity of society: individuals must perpetuate conventions, mores and beliefs in an effort to pass behaviour patterns from generation to generation.

9.3.2 Agencies of socialisation

It is hard to think of an area of our lives untouched by the process of socialisation. Even if we choose not to interact with other people we are in fact still choosing a form of socialisation — that of avoidance. The principal agencies from which we learn socialisation skills are:

(a) **Family:** The family is the strongest socialisation agency. We learn how to cope, share and adjust to life. The familial influence can extend into adulthood, affecting 'life' decisions, such as choice of career, marriage partner. The family is our first introduction into society (the society of our siblings and extended family) and subconsciously we adopt its value system. It serves as a base for later independent functioning and as a touchstone for the development of new relationships.

(b) **School:** After the family we spend most of our formative years in primary and secondary education. Here we get the opportunity to mix with other people, affording us a different perspective on the behaviours and beliefs experienced to date. School is also the setting in which the State first has a chance to influence individuals through its interpretation of the curriculum subjects. It is a potent force in the socialisation of the child, inculcating him with societal attitudes.

(c) **Peer groups:** These are groups of people with whom we identify. They could be friends, work colleagues or associates possessing similar interests, e.g. sports clubs, charities or political groupings. Though the amount of time spent with peer groups is less than with the previous two agencies, they still have influence on us, e.g. teenagers' strict allegiance to dress codes (e.g. jeans) and certain types of music (e.g. rave).

(d) **Mass media:** In this context the mass media refers to the organised means of information transmission through various outlets, such as newspapers, magazines, television, radio and cinema. It is an extremely powerful agency, presenting people with an abundance of alternative lifestyles, beliefs and values. Regardless of our age, mass media continues to exert a strong influence on how we perceive our role within society.

9.3.3 Mechanisms of socialisation

How do we learn socially acceptable behaviours? As we develop through childhood we learn and absorb the rules of appropriate or inappropriate actions. Our behaviour, frequently monitored by family and school, is shaped into a pattern that conforms to society's rules. This process does not cease; throughout our lives we are constantly adapting our behaviours to 'fit in' with the particular social situation. Society's main mechanisms for shaping of behaviour are:

(a) **Imitation:** A young child learns to cope with his environment by imitating his parents; we learn how to act in social settings by imitating the behaviour of those around us, e.g. learning table manners, showing respect to others.

(b) **Conditioning:** This term was last referred to in the context of Behaviourist learning theories (see 3.2), where appropriate behaviour was rewarded and inappropriate behaviour punished. Similarly, our behaviour is conditioned by society's reaction; approval may be encouragement, attention and praise, whilst disapproval may be ostracism, verbal criticism or silence. Similar behavioural treatments from our family/peer groups can also condition our behaviour until we learn to display appropriate and acceptable behaviour.

(c) **Identification:** In the same way that we join certain groups reflecting our views, we also identify with people we feel are similar to ourselves. The most obvious people we identify with are our parents. As we grow older we adopt perceived correct behaviours in accordance with our identification with people such as peers, work colleagues and friends.

9.3.4 Norms

In order to survive and set standards of behaviour, society has evolved its own mechanism for survival, called norms. These important rules of behaviour fulfil two basic functions, they:

(a) **set the standard of behaviour**, dictating what behaviour is acceptable and expected, e.g. when meeting a new acquaintance the norm is to shake hands

(b) **ensure continuity**, i.e. that certain rules of behaviour are repeated by individuals within similar situations.

Norms guide an individual to fit into society and are central to another important aspect of the socialisation process, roles.

9.3.5 Roles

A role may be defined as a pattern of behaviour expected in a specific position, such as teacher, mother, son. We enact several different roles within everyday life, each relevant to a specific social situation. For example, at the moment you are probably in the role of student, during recreation you are a friend, and at home you may be wife, husband, sister, daughter or son. We adopt what we perceive as the behavioural expectations of the particular role we are playing. For example, our behaviour in the role of friend is often different from our behaviour in the role of daughter or son.

Not only do we adopt and enact role expectations, but so too do others; that is to say, others perceiving our behaviour in a specific role often psychologically assess what they would do in similar circumstances. If role perceptions are similar there are no problems, but if perceptions differ, conflict is inevitable. In work situations, for example, an employee who adopts what he considers appropriate behaviour for, say, an assistant, may be at odds with his employer, for the sole reason that the latter possesses different expectations/perceptions for the same role.

Conflicts within role behaviour take two patterns:

(a) **Inter-role conflict:** where performance in one role interferes with performance in another, e.g. a Garda may find that his behaviour at work runs over into his family life and he becomes very autocratic.

(b) **Intra-role conflict:** where conflicting demands of different requirements of the role lead to role ambiguity (confusion) and/or role incompatibility, e.g. where an employee is called on to use his initiative and yet taken to task for not asking permission.

Whatever role we adopt at any particular time is or has been shaped by societal approval. The diagram below displays a simple model of role adoption.

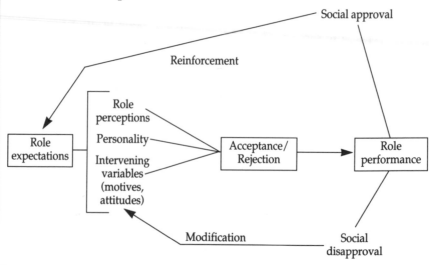

9.3.6 Social class

Social class is hard to define. It exists in all societies and is regarded as a social stratification or ordering method. One definition offered by Schiffman and Kanuk (1987) proposes social class as 'a division of members of a society into a hierarchy of distinct status classes, so that members of each class have relatively the same status and members of all other classes have either more or less status'. In other words, social class is a collection of individuals sharing similar lifestyles and recognising a differentiation between their group and others. This differentiation is regarded as hierarchical, spanning from low to high.

Social class serves as a frame of reference for members and non-members alike, and is perpetuated by the following means:

(a) **Class-Consciousness:** Members of a class are conscious of the existence of shared values, attitudes, beliefs within each class and between social classes.

(b) **Uniformity of lifestyle:** Members within a social class share similar lifestyles, adhering to social expectations, e.g. occupation, education, income levels.

(c) **Patterns of social interaction:** Members share similar behaviour patterns, e.g. areas of social intercourse, recreational pursuits, holidays and residential geography.

9.3.7 Status

Intertwined within the notion of class differentiation is the concept of status. The amount of status possessed by a particular class often defines that class's place in the social hierarchy. Status may be ascribed (given) or achieved (sought) and is often defined in terms of:

(a) wealth/income

(b) power

(c) education

(d) occupation.

These socio-economic variables are recognised and accepted within the class hierarchy as indicators of class positioning. Simply, status is a social identity marker placing people in relation to others.

As we have learned, culture and society shape behaviour, beliefs and values. All cultures possess similar characteristics and components but each is unique in its expression. Our final chapter gives the reader an opportunity to assess the influence of unique forces contributing towards an 'Irish Culture'.

9.4 SUMMARY

1. Culture is the distinctive way of life of a group of people, is learned, serves the needs of society, is cumulative and adaptive.
2. Components of culture are: institutions (conventions, mores and laws), ideas (beliefs, attitudes and values) and materials (technology, arts and literature).
3. The socialisation process prepares an individual for society through the agencies of family, school, peers and media.
4. Mechanisms of society provide a learning framework for appropriate behavioural expressions.
5. Society's norms, roles and social class structures enhance an individual's sense of belonging and identity.

9.5 EXAM QUESTIONS

1. Describe and explain 'culture'.
2. Why is culture considered adaptive?
3. Define what is meant by socialisation and describe the agencies and mechanisms which assist the socialisation process. (MII, 1990)
4. How important are 'norms' in society?
5. Social class has been described as a 'social identity matter'. Would you agree?

Trends in Irish Social Change

10.1   INTRODUCTION
          10.1.1 The background to change in Irish
                society

10.2   THE DEMOGRAPHY OF IRISH SOCIETY
          10.2.1 Emigration

10.3   FERTILITY AND NUPTIALITY

10.4   SOCIAL CLASS
          10.4.1 Preserving the status quo?

10.5   SOCIAL MOBILITY: SOME CONTRIBUTORY
          FACTORS

10.6   AGE AND DEPENDENCY

10.7   CONCLUSION

10.8   SUMMARY

10.9   EXAM QUESTIONS

Learning Objectives

After studying this chapter you should be able to:

— *Present the main demographic changes in Ireland over the last forty years, especially the effect of industrialisation on social class, the family and the distribution of population within the State*
— *Explain how Irish marriage, fertility and mortality rates have changed over the last forty years, and how they compare to the EC average*
— *Discuss what is meant by social class within the Irish context, how it has been affected by industrialisation and how mobile groups are within it*
— *Explain what is meant by the dependency ratio, and what effect it has on the Irish economy and the present age profile of Ireland*
— *Combine the main trends in Irish development over the last forty years to understand the important changes which shape today's society.*

10.1 INTRODUCTION

In many European countries the past exerts a strong 'pull', with events of many years ago still influencing the way the inhabitants act. This is no less true of Ireland, where the past still holds sway over our consciousness and institutions. The reasons for this are many, and are the stuff of both cliché and historical fact.

In this chapter we present a very brief overview of Irish society during the past forty years. Due to the scope of the book, we have simplified — and in some cases omitted — sociological conceptual models. We would encourage the reader with any interest in sociological change to avail of the excellent references for this chapter.

Causes for change in Irish society range from our admission into the EEC and our increasing industrialisation to the lessening in influence of the Roman Catholic Church. The sociological changes, seldom simple, are often the result of complex, long-standing and interactive social forces, such as demography, fertility and nuptiality (marriage).

'Ireland' and 'Irish society' here refer only to the Republic of Ireland. This is for practical reasons as the two Irish entities (north and south) have developed separately and differently over much of this century.

10.1.1 The background to change in Irish society

As Rottman and O'Connell (1982) point out, Irish society has been predominantly rurally based for the main part of the twentieth century. Large numbers of Irish were employed on the land, whether on their own farms or those of others, or as agricultural suppliers of some sort. With the advent of industrialisation this changed, as we discuss later in the chapter. Another fundamental change has been the position of the Roman Catholic Church in Irish society, as described in Breen et al. (1990). A Papal Nuncio once described Ireland as the most Catholic country in the world, and this was reflecting the fact that Irish social legislation mirrored the Church's position on most social issues. This has altered in the last thirty years, with particularly significant changes, and attempted changes, in the late 1980s. Such moves have had a knock-on effect on the structure of the Irish family, as noted by Kennedy (1986).

Finally, as a background to Irish society, the eventual admission of Ireland to the EEC, now the European Union (formerly the EC), has led to the implementation of economic and social directives which have forced changes in every section of Irish society.

10.2 THE DEMOGRAPHY OF IRISH SOCIETY

Demographics is the study of population movement, usually within the confines of a particular state. It includes migration (movement within a state), emigration (movement out of a state) and immigration (movement into a state). We discuss the demography within the Irish State during the last forty years or so.

Ever since the Famine, Ireland has had a reputation for large-scale emigration of its population to countries with a greater supply of employment. This has been the most characteristic and best-known demographic factor in Irish society. However, it obscures the very important factor of migration. We examine first the reasons for, and effect of, migration in Irish society.

Up to and including the 1950s, Ireland was economically dependent on its trade with Britain, and its fortunes were often those of Britain. Ireland was a hostage to the state of the British economy. The 1950s were an especially bad time for the Republic, with a severely depressed Irish economy and high emigration to Britain. Through the First Programme for Economic Expansion, in 1958, the Irish Government sought to lessen its reliance on Britain by propagating investment from foreign multinationals and embracing the industrialisation spreading throughout the Western world. The result of the First and Second Programmes for Economic Expansion (the latter in 1964) was the setting up of such bodies as the Industrial Development Authority, the National Economic and Social Council, and the Economic and Social Research Institute in the late 1950s and early 1960s. The two National Expansion programmes tackled the large-scale emigration and unemployment problems and their efforts were to have a major effect on migration patterns within the Republic, particularly the concentration of population on the eastern seaboard. Industrial development in the eastern region of Ireland (i.e. Meath, Kildare, Wicklow and Dublin) led to a large population movement to that area in order to fill the jobs being created. By the 1980s, 30 per cent of the nation's population would live in this area surrounding the capital.

This population explosion in the Greater Dublin area, and its surrounding counties, led to the burgeoning satellite towns (e.g. Tallaght, Finglas), and to the decline of the inner-city areas of Dublin and other cities. The net effect was that groups such as teenagers, single people and the economically deprived were more vulnerable to migration. This movement led to a depletion in the numbers working in agriculture, and, as a consequence, a decrease in the importance of this sector for Irish culture and economy. This migration pattern is in line with other European countries, but as Courtney (1982) has noted, is low by international standards.

10.2.1 Emigration

For many people the spectacle of emigration is more emotive and often of greater concern than the less-mentioned migration. At the beginning of the period we are examining, i.e. the 1950s, there was a great deal of emigration from Ireland to Britain. The problem was examined by the Commission on Emigration, in 1955, and attempts were made to alleviate it by the First and Second Programmes for Economic Expansion (1958, 1964).

As a result of the ensuing industrialisation and an upturn in the world economy in the 1960s, emigration decreased and immigration increased, i.e. people returning to live in Ireland. However, owing to the depressed state of the 1970s world economy and synchronous with an increase in the Irish population, the numbers emigrating rose once again. This was reversed in the early 1980s with a net inflow, or a majority of immigration over emigration, caused less by an improvement of Irish and world economies during the early 1980s than by the lack of work opportunities abroad, where previously they had existed. It was believed better to come home to Ireland than be unemployed abroad. This had a concomitant effect on the level of unemployment, and the amount the Government had to set aside for social welfare. Further, it has placed an onus on future governments to increase the number of jobs created.

10.3 FERTILITY AND NUPTIALITY

Due to the predominance of land in Irish society, and the succession rights therein, Ireland has had a traditionally late marriage age and a high level of celibacy. Daughters within a family were often married off with a dowry, and those sons not in a position to inherit would often emigrate. Even those who did inherit frequently waited till both parents died. Where the mother was some years younger than the father — as was often the case in Ireland — the son was into middle age before he married; thus it was a self-perpetuating phenomenon.

Other traditional factors contributing to this unique nuptial pattern were high levels of marital fertility, meaning the number of children born to each marriage. As only the eldest son inherited, the others had to seek a living in the locality (of which there was little chance), in the industrialised east of the country or by emigrating.

The changes of the last three decades were gradual and complex, and their manner could hardly have been foreseen, but they radically altered the fertility and nuptiality patterns within Irish society.

Between the years 1961 and 1981 there was a drop in marital fertility in Ireland. Courtney (1982) suggests the following reasons:

(a) During this period there were substantial occupational changes from agriculture into production and service industries, coupled with increasing regional development and urbanisation. This had the effect of moving more people from the land, and from the implicit acceptance that they would adopt traditional roles within marriage.

(b) There was an increase of married women within the workforce. Up to 1973 there was what was known as the 'Civil Service ban' on married women in the workforce. This meant that once women in certain occupations married, they had to give up their jobs and stay in the home. This situation first showed signs of changing in 1967, when banks removed the ban on married women working. The real catalyst, however, was Ireland's accession to the EEC in 1973, and the equality directives it subsequently adopted. These changed society's perceptions of women — and women's rights — in the workplace.

(c) The changes in the law on contraception came soon after a restating of the Roman Catholic Church's views on the subject in the encyclical *Humanae Vitae* (1967). This combined with the increasingly vocal views of feminists, represented by Greer (1967), that women could have control over their lives only when they had control over their fertility. It was in this atmosphere of change and questioning of moral values that a concerted campaign began to force a change in the Republic's contraceptive laws. Campaigners had long been making frequent and well-publicised trips to Northern Ireland with its more liberal contraceptive laws, attempting to goad the Republic's authorities into changing legislation by openly flaunting the law.

The McGee case (1973) came to the Supreme Court, where Mrs McGee argued through her lawyers that the law should be interpreted to allow the import of contraceptives — the law up to then actually banning their *importation*. Mrs McGee won her case and the Government was forced to bring a bill before the Oireachtas providing for the importation of contraceptives. This bill (1973) and the subsequent 1979 Act restricted the availability of contraceptives to married couples, and then when prescribed by a medical practitioner. It was only in 1986 that chemists were permitted to supply contraceptives. The 1992 and 1993 Acts ultimately led to a liberalising of the provision of vending-machines for condoms and a lowering of the age at which contraceptives could be prescribed or sold. All of this has contributed to a drop in the fertility of women.

(d) As Kennedy (1986) points out, the increasing influence of television on our lives and the greater receptivity to ideas due to our EEC membership meant that people in Ireland began to live differently. Further, they began to embrace different moral values from those advocated by the Church. This has led, amongst other things, to an increase in the number of children born outside marriage and in the number of couples prepared to live together outside marriage.

Although our pattern of fertility and nuptiality is moving towards the European norm, Courtney (1982) states that the Irish pattern is 'still quite distinctive' in that the average age at marriage and size of family remains higher than those of our European neighbours. Fertility and nuptiality changes in our society have exerted strong influences on the Irish family. Along with changes in contraception, removal of the Civil Service ban and EC equality directives, there is a recognition on the part of the State of the role of women in society. This has helped to allow women the choice of working inside or outside the home and, as Kennedy remarks, has substantially changed the nature of the family in Ireland. The Irish family has not been immune to the pan-European sociological change — from extended to nuclear family — but it has received little or no support from the State, in line with the State's constitutional duty to do so (Kennedy, 1986). This, in addition to the industrialisation of the last forty years, means that the Irish family is not the primary unit of socialisation it used to be.

10.4 SOCIAL CLASS

Social class is a term used to describe an individual according to his income level or interests. It is an emotive term because the suggestion that someone is from a particular social class often has disparaging resonances and implications.

We examine here the effect social class has had on Irish society in the last forty years and the influence on class structure of the changes previously discussed; whether, for example, it has been transformed by industrialisation. More importantly, we examine how the social class system treats its members in the sense of allowing them to move upwards or downwards — in other words, social mobility.

10.4.1 Preserving the status quo?

Whelan and Whelan (1985) seek to present the case that Irish social class structures are quite rigid in that they have not allowed for social mobility. They state:

> What we can say is that only 1 in 20 moved from manual origins to the professional and managerial class while a mere 2 per cent of those with fathers in the latter class were currently in manual work. Movement from rags to riches is rarer than movement from rags to relative affluence, but a great deal more common than movement from riches to rags.

Whelan and Whelan note that it has been a characteristic of the Irish social class system that 'manual' workers find it harder to progress through the social hierarchy than 'the immediate non-manual class' or those born in 'the professional and managerial class'. They go on to examine, as will we, the reasons for this persistent lack of social mobility, the ways in which it might be alleviated and whether it has changed in any way over the last few decades.

10.5 SOCIAL MOBILITY: SOME CONTRIBUTORY FACTORS

Education is, theoretically, a strong enabler of social mobility, allowing movement between social classes on the basis of acquisition of primary, secondary and third-level education. This vocational training (such as medicine, commerce, science and arts) has a greater societal value, in terms of potential remuneration, than manual and unskilled work. Accordingly, those individuals who pursue it are more likely to earn more and to attain a higher social class.

Although there are State grants to encourage those from deprived backgrounds to enter the later stages of the educational process — i.e. third level — they have not done so in comparable numbers to those from middle-class backgrounds. This is in spite of the fact that since 1967 education in Ireland has been nominally free, with the then Minister for Education, Donagh O'Malley, providing free transport and secondary schooling. The aim was to facilitate participation of those from the lower social classes, whose involvement in the educational system ceased once they reached the legal age for leaving school. Their departure was often due to the economic necessity of additional income for the family and to the discouraging prospect of expenditure on secondary — let alone third-level — education.

The effect of this 'free' education (it was not fully free, in that books, school uniforms and other unforeseen items were not included) was to increase the number of fifteen-year-olds still at school from less than half to over 85 per cent between 1965 and 1979. However, it was still the case in the early 1980s that those from a more deprived background were more likely to leave school without any qualifications. As Whelan and Whelan (1985) state:

> At second level, it has been estimated that boys from upper non-manual families are at least six times more likely to sit for the leaving certificate than are those whose father is an unskilled or semi-skilled manual worker. Furthermore, they are almost thirteen times more likely to enter third-level education.

The consequence is those leaving school without any qualification are more likely to be unemployed than those who leave school with a Leaving Certificate. However, the opportunity of increased educational participation *per se* does not necessarily increase the chances that individuals from deprived backgrounds will remain in the educational system.

While industrialisation and an upturn in the world economy in the 1960s allowed Ireland to finance the provision of a 'free' educational system, it has not led to a significant amount of social mobility. Those from less skilled and more deprived classes are more prone to unemployment owing to their lack of qualifications. They have also been traditionally more prone to emigration. Industrialisation has meant that Ireland's class system has stayed largely intact, with the more economically advantaged classes benefiting from the provision of education. Little movement upwards has occurred from the unskilled manual classes, whose members are also less likely to marry and more likely to be the victims of infant mortality.

10.6 AGE AND DEPENDENCY

This section looks at Ireland's age profile and its effect on 'dependency' needs. Dependency refers to those who have to be supported by the State either because they cannot do so themselves or because they are not yet in a position to do so, e.g. children and the elderly.

Ireland differs in age profile from its European counterparts, with 16,000 more males than females, and more females than males over the age of sixty-five. The excess of males over females is partly attributable to the fact that more females than males emigrated in the last few decades.

Another aspect of Ireland's age profile is that in the early 1980s roughly a third of the Irish population was under the age of twenty-five. The effect of this, combined with the high number over sixty-five, is that there is a large group of people dependent on the State. This means that the 'dependency ratio' (those under fifteen and over sixty-five) on persons in economically productive groups is quite high. In fact, according to Courtney (1982), it has increased since the 1950s and is higher than the EC average (53 per 100 as opposed to our 69 per 100). This has important implications for public expenditure because of increases in unemployment benefit and old age social welfare.

10.7 CONCLUSION

Over the last several decades Ireland has witnessed sweeping changes in its economic, social and demographic patterns to such an extent that the rural Ireland of the early part of this century is no more. In its place is a modern, technologically advanced, well educated population residing mainly in urban areas. Contributing factors included industrialisation, the decreasing influence of the

Catholic Church, technological advancements such as television, of the role of women and restructuring of changes in family unit. The Ireland of today is more outward-looking than before and more responsive to the needs of a modern dynamic society.

10.8 SUMMARY

1. Ireland has a very distinctive pattern of emigration, due to a lack of employment prospects. This has been halted in the 1980s, due to returning emigrants.
2. Ireland has a pattern of migration similar to other European countries, which emerged with the increasing industrialisation of the State from the early 1950s. Fewer people are employed in the agricultural sector, and a great deal more in industry. This has resulted in people moving to the east of the country, which now has approximately 30 per cent of the population.
3. Ireland's pattern of fertility and nuptiality is slowly moving towards the European norm, although average age at marriage and size of family remains higher.
4. Ireland has a fairly rigid and structured class system which does not permit social mobility.
5. Ireland possesses a high dependency ratio in comparison to its European counterparts.

10.9 EXAM QUESTIONS

1. To what extent does social class influence family structure and life chances in Ireland? (MII, 1991)
2. Outline the principal determinants of demographic change and show how they currently affect Irish population structure. (MII, 1992)
3. Outline the principal changes in Irish family demography since 1960. Why have these changes taken place? (MII, 1991)
4. Discuss the reasons why many commentators claim that Irish social class differences are as pronounced today as they were thirty years ago. (MII, 1991)
5. Assess the impact of economic and industrial development since 1950 on Ireland's class structure. (MII, 1990)

REFERENCES

CHAPTER 1

Boring, E.G. (1928) (1982) in D. Schultz, *A History of Modern Psychology*, 3rd ed. (New York: Academic Press).

Chisnall, P. (1985), *Marketing: A Behavioural Analysis*, 2nd ed. (Maidenhead: McGraw-Hill).

Coon, D. (1986), *Introduction to Psychology* (St Paul: West Publishing).

Francis, A. (1988), *Business Mathematics and Statistics*, 2nd ed. (Hampshire: DP Publications).

Hair, J.F. jr, Anderson, R.E., Tatham, R.L. and Black, W.C. (1992), *Multivariate Data Analysis* (New York: Maxwell Macmillan).

James, H. (1890), *The Science of Mental Life* (Boston: Harvard University Press).

CHAPTER 2

Best, J.B. (1986), *Cognitive Psychology* (St Paul: West Publishing).

Kelley, H.H. (1980) in B. Weiner (ed.), *Human Motivation* (New York: Holt, Rinehart and Winston).

Kretch, D., Crutchfield, R.S. and Ballachey, E.L. (1962), *The Individual in Society* (New York: McGraw-Hill).

Leeper, R.W. (1935), 'A study of a neglected portion of the field of learning. The development of sensory organisation', *Pedagogical Seminary and Journal of Genetic Psychology*, 46, 41–75.

Langer, E.J. and Abelson, R.P. (1974), 'A patient by any other name. Clinician group differences in labelling bias', *Journal of Consulting and Clinical Psychology*, 42, 4–9.

Rothbart, M. and Birrell, P. (1977), 'Attitude and the perception of faces', *Journal of Research Personality*, 11, 209–15.

Steers, R.M. (1991), *Introduction to Organisational Behaviour* (New York: Harper Collins).

Webster, F. (1987), 'Decision making in the employment interview' in T.R. Mikell and J.R. Larson (eds.) (1987), *People in Organisations* (New York: McGraw-Hill).

CHAPTER 3

Atkinson, R.C. and Shiffrin, R.M. (1971), 'The control of short term memory', *Scientific American*, 224.

Coon, D. (1986), *Introduction to Psychology* (St Paul: West Publishing).

Kohler, W. (1925), *The Mentality of Apes* (New York: Harcourt Brace).

Millar, G. (1956), 'Learning' in D. Wright and A. Taylor (eds.) (1978), *Introductory Psychology: An Experimental Approach* (UK: Penguin Education).

Pavlov, I.P. (1927), *Conditioned Reflexes* (London: Oxford University Press).

Skinner, B.F. (1953), *Science and Human Behaviour* (New York: Macmillan).

Tolman, E.C. (1939), *Purposive Behaviour in Animals and Men* (New York: Appleton-Century-Crofts).

CHAPTER 4

Adams, J.S. (1965), 'Injustice in social exchange' in L. Berkowitz (ed.) (1975), *Advances in Experimental Social Psychology* (New York: Academic Press).

Buchanan, D. and Huczynski, A. (1991), *Organizational Behaviour*, 2nd ed. (London: Prentice Hall).

Galbraith, J. and Cummings, L.L. (1967), 'An empirical investigation of the motivational determinants of task performance', *Organizational Behaviour and Human Performance*, vol. 2, 237–57.

Herzberg, F., Mausner, B. and Synderman, B.B. (1959), *The Motivation to Work*, 2nd ed. (New York: Chapman and Hall).

Herzberg, F. (1974), *Work and the Nature of Man* (London: Granada Publishing).

Maslow, A.H. (1968), *Toward a Psychology of Being*, 2nd ed. (Princeton, NJ: D. Van Nostrand).

McClelland, D.C. (1961), *The Achieving Society* (New York: Free Press).

McGregor, D. (1960), *The Human Side of Enterprise* (New York: McGraw-Hill).

Taylor, F.W. (1947), *Scientific Management* (New York: Harper & Row).

Vroom, V.H. (1964), *Work and Motivation* (New York: Wiley).

Vroom, V.H. and Deci, E.L. (1970), *Management and Motivation* (Harmondsworth: Penguin).

Williams, K. (1981), *Behavioural Aspects of Marketing* (UK: Redwood).

CHAPTER 5

Allport, G.W. (1954), *The Nature of Prejudice* (Reading, Massachusetts: Addison-Wesley).

Bogardus, E.S. (1925), 'Measuring social distance', *Journal of Applied Sociology*, 9, 299–308.

Festinger, L. (1957), *A Theory of Cognitive Dissonance* (New York: Harper & Row).

Fishbein, M. (1967), 'Attitudes and Prediction of Behaviour' in M. Fishbein (ed.), *Attitudes, Theory and Measurement* (New York: Wiley).

Fishbein, M. and Azjen, I. (1975), *Belief, Attitude, Intention and Behaviour* (Reading, Mass.: Addison-Wesley).

Guttman, L. (1950), 'The basis for scalogram analysis' in S.A. Stouffer (ed.) (Princeton, NJ: Princeton University Press).

Heider, F. (1958), *The Psychology of Interpersonal Relations* (New York: Wiley).

Heider, F. (1946), 'Attitudes and cognitive organization', *Journ. Psychology*, 21.

Katz, D. (1960), 'The functional approach to the study of attitudes', *Public Opinion Quarterly*, 24, 163–204.

Kretch, D., Crutchfield, R.S. and Ballachey, E.L. (1962), *The Individual in Society* (New York: McGraw-Hill).

Likert, R. (1932), 'A technique for the measurement of attitudes', *Archives of Psychology*, 22, 140.

Loudon, D. and Della Butta, A. (1993), *Consumer Behaviour: Concepts & Applications* (New York: McGraw-Hill).

Osgood, C.E., Suci, G.J. and Tannenbaum, P.H. (1957), *The Measurement of Meaning* (Urbana, Illinois: University of Illinois Press).

Thurstone, L.L. and Chave, E.J. (1929), *Primary Mental Attitudes* (Chicago: University of Chicago Press).

CHAPTER 6

Cattell, R.B. (1983) *Structured Personality-Learning Theory* (New York: Praeger).

Freud, S. (1964), *New Introductory Lectures on Psychoanalysis*, in standard edition, vol. 22 (London: Hogarth Press) (first German edition, 1933).

Gross, R.D. (1992), *Psychology: The Science of Mind and Behaviour* (London: Hodder and Stoughton).

Jung, C.G. (1971), *Psychological Types*, in *Collected Works*, vol. 6 (Princeton, NJ: Princeton University Press) (first German edition, 1921).

Rogers, C.R. (1961), *On Becoming a Person* (Boston: Houghton Mifflin).

CHAPTER 7

Asch, S. (1956), 'Studies of independence and conformity' in R.M. Steers (ed.) (1991), *Introduction to Organisational Behaviour* (New York: Harper Collins).

Buchanan, D. and Huczynski, A. (1991), *Organisational Behaviour*, 2nd ed. (London: Prentice Hall).

Festinger, L. (1950), 'Informal social communication', *Psychological Review* (1983), September, 275.

Hackman, J. and Morris, C. (1975), 'Group tasks, group interaction process & group performance effectiveness' in L. Berkowitz (ed.), *Advances in Experimental Social Psychology* (New York: Academic Press).

Hall, G. and Lindzey, G. (1985), *Introduction to Theories of Personality* (New York: Wiley).

Kiesler, C.A. and Kiesler, S.B. (1969), 'Conformity' in D.G. Myers (ed.) (1990), *Social Psychology* (New York: McGraw-Hill).

Loudon, D. and Della Butta, A. (1993), *Consumer Behaviour: Concepts & Applications* (New York: McGraw-Hill).

Milgram, S. (1974), *Obedience to Authority* (New York: Harper & Row).

Morris, W. and Miller, R.S. (1975), 'The effect of consensus-breaking and consensus-pre-empting partners on reduction of conformity' in D.G. Myers (ed.) (1990), *Social Psychology* (New York: McGraw-Hill).

Moorhead, G. and Griffin, R. (1992), *Organisational Behaviour*, 3rd ed. (Boston: Houghton Mifflin).

Mullen, B. (1985), 'Strength and immediacy of sources', *Journal of Personality and Social Psychology*, 48, 1458–66.

Sherif, M. and Sherif, C. (1969), *Social Psychology* (New York: Harper & Row).

Tuckman, B and Jenson, M. (1977), 'Stages of small group development revisited', *Groups and Organisational Studies*, 2, 419–42.

CHAPTER 8

Davis, K. and Newstrom, J. (1985), *Human Behaviour at Work: Organisational Behaviour*, 7th ed. (New York: McGraw-Hill).

Katz, D. and Kahn, R.L. (1978), *The Social Psychology of Organisations*, 2nd ed. (New York: Liviley).

Moorhead, G. and Griffin, R. (1992), *Organisational Behaviour*, 3rd ed. (Boston: Houghton Mifflin).

Nicholas, R. (1962), 'Listening is good business', in R.M. Steers (ed.) (1991), *Introduction to Organisational Behaviour* (New York: Harper Collins).

O'Reilly, C. and Pondy, L.R. (1979), 'Organisational communication' in Moorhead and Griffin (eds.), *Organisational Behaviour* (Boston: Houghton Mifflin).

Snyder, R. and Morris, J. (1984), 'Organisational communication and performance', *Journal of Applied Psychology*, August, 461–5.

Trist, E. and Banforth, K. (1951), 'Some social and psychological consequences of the long-wall method of coal getting', *Human Relations*, February.

CHAPTER 9

Fanning, R. (1983), *Independent Ireland* (Dublin: Helicon Ltd).

Kluckhohn, C. (1951) in D. Loudon and A. Della Butta (eds.) (1993), *Consumer Behaviour: Concepts & Applications* (New York: McGraw-Hill).

Yussen, S. and Santrock, J. (1987), *Child Development: An Introduction* (New Jersey: Prentice Hall).

Schiffman, L.G. and Kanuk, L.L. (1991), *Consumer Behaviour*, 4th ed. (Englewood Cliffs, NJ: Prentice-Hall).

CHAPTER 10

Breen, R., Hannan, D.F., Rottman, D.B. and Whelan, C.T. (1990), *Understanding Contemporary Ireland* (Dublin: Gill and Macmillan).

Courtney, D. (1982) in Patrick Clancy (ed.), *Ireland: A Sociological Profile* (Dublin: Institute of Public Administration in association with the Sociological Association of Ireland).

Fanning, R. (1983), *Independent Ireland* (Dublin: Helicon Ltd).

Greer, G. (1967), *The Female Eunuch* (London: Pan).

Kennedy, F. (1986), 'The family in transition' in K.A. Kennedy (ed.), *Ireland in Transition: Economic and Social Change* (Dublin: Mercier).

Rottman, D.B. and O'Connell, P.J. (1982), 'The changing social structure of Ireland' in F. Litton (ed.), *Unequal Achievement: The Irish Experience 1957–1982* (Dublin: Institute of Public Administration).

Whelan, C.T. and Whelan, B.J. (1985), 'Equality of opportunity in Irish schools: a reassessment', *Economic and Social Review*, 16 (2), 103–14.

INDEX

absolute threshold, 20
achievement, need for, 67–8
Adams, J.S., 73–4, 142
affective component, 84
Allport, Gordon, 79
altered illumination effects, 140–41
anthropology, 4
Asch, Soloman, 138
association
    conditioning, 42–4
Atkinson and Shiffrin memory model,
    51–3
attitude change
    message factors, 100–101
    receiver factors, 101–2
    source factors, 100
attitude measurement, 85–91
    Likert scale, 88–90
    Scalogram Analysis, 90–91
    semantic differential scale, 86–7
    Thurstone scale, 88
attitudes, 78–102
    attitude change, 99–102
    and behaviour, 84–5
    characteristics of, 80–81
    consistency models, 91–5
    functions of, 81–2
    measurement. see attitude
        measurement
    possible definitions, 79–81
    post-purchase dissonance theories,
        95–9
    sources of, 82–3
    tricomponent attitude model, 83–4
attribution, 31–2
attribution bias, 37
augmented product or service, 3
Auto-Kinetic Effect, 132
Azjen, I., 97

balance theory, 91–3
behavioural science
    definition of, 4–7

methods of studying, 7–14
problems of, 12–14
reasons for studying, 2–3
vs. natural science, 6–7
Behaviourist School, 41–7
    classical conditioning, 42–4
    evaluation, 46–7
    operant conditioning, 44–6
beliefs, 79–80
body language, 34
Bogardus, E.S., 90
Boring, E.G., 6
bureaucracy, 149–50

case-study method, 8
Cattell, Raymond, 107, 119
    personality theories, 115–18
class, social, 177
    in Ireland, 185–6
    social mobility, 186–8
classical conditioning, 42–4
classical organisation theory, 149
closure, law of, 28
cognitive component, 84
cognitive dissonance theory, 93–4
Cognitive Learning Theories, 47–50
    evaluation, 49
    insight learning, 48
    latent learning, 49
common goals, 148
communication, 157–63
    all-channel network, 163
    chain network, 162
    circle network, 163
    feedback variable, 159–60
    organisational variables, 160–63
    receiver variable, 159
    sender variable, 158–9
    wheel network, 162
compensatory mechanisms, 155
conative component, 84
conformity research, 137–40
congruity theory, 94–5

Connectionist School. *see* Behaviourist
      School
consistency models
      balance theory, 91–3
      cognitive dissonance theory, 93–4
      congruity theory, 94–5
consumerism
      and behavioural science, 2–3
      and perception, 18
content theories of motivation, 63–71
      Herzberg's theory, 69–71
      Maslow's theory, 64–6
      McClelland's theory, 67–8
      McGregor's theory, 68–9
Contingency theory, 151
Courtney, D., 182, 184, 185
Critical Incident Technique, 69–71
'cues', 22
culture, 170–73
      characteristics of, 171
      components of, 172–3
      expressions of, 170
      and society, 169–78
      subcultures, 170–71

defence mechanisms, 112
demography
      of Irish society, 181–3
denial, 119
dependency ratio, 188
dependent variables, 5
differential threshold, 20–21
dissonance theory, 93–4
division of labour, 148
drives
      positive and negative, 60
      unlearned and learned, 59–60

economics, 4
education
      and social mobility, 186–7
Ego, 108–12
emigration, 182–3
equity theory, 73–4
European Community (EC), 180, 181,
      184, 185
expectancy theory, 71–3
experimental method, 9

external attribution, 31–2
external cues, 22–3
external validity, 10–11
extinction, 43–4
extroversion, 114

Fayol, Henri, 149
fertility, 183–5
Festinger, Leon, 93
figure-ground, law of, 26
first impressions, 36–7
Fishbein, M., 95–9
      extended model, 97–9
      first model, 96–7
Freud, Sigmund, 8, 61, 119
      idiographic approach, 107
      personality theories, 107–13
frustration, responses to, 61–2

Gestalt, 169
      laws of, 25–8
group structure, 128–33
      cohesiveness, 128–9
      communication, 132–3
      norms, 131–2
      roles, 130–31
      size, 133
      status, 129–30
grouping, law of, 27
groups, 122–42. *see also* group structure
      categorisations of, 126–8
      conformity research, 137–40
      definition of, 123
      development of, 133–6
      Forming, Storming, Norming,
            Performing, 133–6
      Hawthorne Studies, 140–42
      power of, 136–42
      reasons for joining, 124–5
      reference group, 127–8
Guttman, L., 90–91

halo effect, 36
Hawthorne Studies, 140–42
Heider, F., 91
Herzberg, Frederick, 64, 69–71
hierarchy of authority, 148
Hierarchy of Needs, 64–6

higher order conditioning, 44
homoeostasis, 59
human relations theory, 152–3
Human Resource Management (HRM), 69

Id, 108–12
idiographic approach, 106–7
implicit personality theory, 36
incongruency, 119
independent variables, 5
individual's perceptual world
    attribution, 31–2
    categorisation, 29
    perceptual defence, 30–31
    perceptual expectancies, 29–30
    selective perception, 30
industrialisation, 180, 181
    and social mobility, 187–8
insight learning, 48
internal attribution, 31
internal cues, 23–4
internal validity, 10
interval scale, 11–12
introversion, 114
Ireland
    social change, 180–89

James, Henry, 169
Jung, Carl Gustav, 75, 107
    personality theories, 113–15
Just Noticeable Difference (JND), 20–21

Katz, Daniel, 81, 99
Kohler, Wolfgang, 48, 50
Kretch, D. and Crutchfield, R.S., 79
Kretch, D., Crutchfield, R.S. and
        Ballachey, E.L., 79

latent learning, 49
learning, 40–50
    Behaviourist School, 41–7
    Cognitive Learning Theories, 47–50
    comparison between theories, 50
    definition, 41
Likert, R., 87, 88–90
line experiment, 138
logos, 24
long-term memory, 52, 53

McClelland, David C., 63, 67–8
McGee case, 184–5
McGregor, D., 64, 68–9
management. see also scientific
        management
    and behavioural science, 3
    and perception, 18
market research, 90–91
marketing
    perception, 18
Maslow, Abraham, 63, 64–6, 107
Mayo, Elton, 140–42
measurement. see scales of
        measurement
memory, 50–54
    Atkinson and Shiffrin model, 51–3
    and forgetting, 53–4
    functions of, 50–51
    improving, 54
methodologies, 8–10
migration, 181–2
Milgram, Stanley, 139–40
mnemonics, 54
Moral Principle, 108
motivation, 57–75
    basic and associated concepts, 57–8
    content theories, 63–71
    definition, 58
    drives, 59–60
    process theories of, 71–4
    research, 74–5
    responses to frustration, 61–2
    state and trait motivation, 58–9
    traditional motivational theory, 62–3

natural science
    vs. behavioural science, 6–7
need, theories of, 64–71
negative reinforcement, 45
Nicholas, Ralph, 160
nominal scale, 11
nomothetic approach, 106–7
non-verbal communication, 34
nuptiality, 183–5

obedience study, 139–40
O'Malley, Donagh, 187
operant conditioning, 44–6

ordinal scale, 11
organisational experience, 147–57
    concepts, 147–9
    theoretical approaches, 149–54
organisational motivation, 68–71
organisations, 145–66. *see also*
        organisational experience
    change, 164–6
    communication, 157–63
    definition of, 147
    Gestalt, 145–6
    interaction between human and
        organisational behaviour,
        157–66
    psychological contract, 166
    recruitment, 155–7
    technology, 154–5
    theoretical approaches
        classical approach, 149
        human relations approach,
            152–3
        systems approach, 150–52
        Weber's Bureaucracy, 149–50
Osgood, C.E., 86–7, 94

Pavlov, Ivan, 41, 42–4, 50
perception, 17–38
    individual's perceptual world,
        29–32
    perceptual organisation, 25–8
    perceptual selectivity, 21–4
    sensation, 19–21
    social perception, 32–8
perceptual defence, 30–31
perceptual organisation, 25–8
perceptual selectivity, 21–4
    external cues, 22–3
    internal cues, 23–4
    selection process, 21–2
personality, 105–19
    definition of, 106
    theories and theorists, 115–18
        Freud, 107–13
        Jung, 113–15
        Rogers, 118–19
personality beliefs, 36
physical appearance, 33
Pleasure Principle, 108

positive reinforcement, 45
process theories of motivation, 71–4
    equity theory, 73–4
    expectancy theory, 71–3
projection, 36
psychology, 4, 90
    motivation research, 74–5
psychometric method, 8–9

quantitative and qualitative research, 5
questionnaires, 75

racism, 171
ratio scale, 11–12
Reality Principle, 108
recruitment
    classification approach, 156–7
    selection approach, 155–6
reference group, 127–8
research
    forming the question, 7–8
    methodologies, 8–10
    quantitative and qualitative, 5
    questionnaires, 75
    scales of measurement, 11–12
    validity, 10–11
Rogers, Carl, 107
    personality theories, 118–19
Roman Catholic Church, 180, 181, 184
Rorschach Test, 75

sampling, 5
scales
    differences among, 85–6
    differential and summational, 86
    manifest or latent, 86
    of measurement, 11–12
science
    goals of, 6–7
scientific management, 149
    Taylor's principles, 62–3, 68–9
selective perception, 30
self-concept theory, 118–19
sensation, 19–21
    habituation, 21
    thresholds, 20–21
sensory memory, 51
Sherif, Muzafer, 132

short-term memory, 51–2
Skinner, B.F., 41, 44–6, 50
social change
    age and dependency, 188
    background to, 181
    demography, 181–3
    fertility and nuptiality, 183–5
    in Ireland, 180–89
    social class, 185–6
    social mobility, 186–8
social perception, 32–8
    characteristics of perceiver, 34–5
    characteristics of person perceived,
        33–4
    characteristics of situation, 35
    influencing factors, 35–7
    views of others, 32–3
society, 173–8. see also social change
    agencies of socialisation, 173–4
    mechanisms of socialisation, 174–5
    norms, 175
    roles, 175–6
    social class, 177
    socialisation, 173
    status, 177–8
Socio-Technical systems theory, 152
sociology, 4
source traits, 116
spontaneous recovery, 44
state motivation, 58–9
statistical analysis, 8
stereotyping, 36
stimulus generalisation, 43

Super-Ego, 108–12
surface traits, 116
survey method, 9
synergy, 122
systematic observation, 8
systems theory, 150–52

Taylor, F.W., 62–3, 68–9
television, 185
temperature scales, 12
Thematic Apperception Test (TAT), 75
Theory X and Theory Y, 68–9
Thorndike, E.L., 41
Thurstone, L.L. and Chave, E.J., 88
Tolman, Edward C., 49, 50
trait motivation, 59
tricomponent attitude model, 83–4
Tuckman, B., 134–6

validity, 10–11
values, 79–80
variable
    definition of, 4–5
verbal communication, 34
Vroom, V.H., 71–3, 142

Waldheim, Kurt, 30
Watson, John, 41
Weber, Max, 149
Weber's Bureaucracy, 149–50
Weber's Law, 20–21
Word Association Test, 75
work, motivation for, 68–71